9 STEP
NEGATIVITY
DETOX

Hardie Grant

BOOKS

DOMONIQUE BERTOLUCCI

9 STEP NEGATIVITY DETOX

RESET YOUR MINDSET and LOVE YOUR LIFE

Published in 2022 by Hardie Grant Books, an imprint of Hardie Grant Publishing

Hardie Grant Books (Melbourne)
Wurundjeri Country
Building 1, 658 Church Street
Richmond, Victoria 3121

Hardie Grant Books (London)
5th & 6th Floors
52–54 Southwark Street
London SE1 1UN

hardiegrantbooks.com

A catalogue record for this
book is available from the
National Library of Australia

9 Step Negativity Detox: Reset your mindset and love your life
ISBN 978 1 74379 803 4

10 9 8 7 6 5 4 3 2 1

Publisher: Pam Brewster
Project Editor: Brooke Munday
Editor: Kate Daniel
Design Manager: Kristin Thomas
Designer: Regine Abos
Typesetter: Kirbyjones
Production Manager: Todd Reichner
Production Coordinator: Jessica Harvie

Colour reproduction by Splitting Image Colour Studio
Printed in China by Leo Paper Products LTD.

Hardie Grant acknowledges the Traditional Owners of the country on which we work, the Wurundjeri people of the Kulin nation and the Gadigal people of the Eora nation, and recognises their continuing connection to the land, waters and culture. We pay our respects to their Elders past and present.

✳

For Sophia and Tobias

✴

*Most people are nowhere near as happy or satisfied with
their lives as they could be and as they should be. They
feel weighed down by stress and pressure, held back by
judgement and lack of opportunity and constantly criticised
by everyone – unfortunately, this includes themselves.*

*If that sounds like you, I want you to know that as
imperfect as your life might be, things are nowhere near
as bad as you think. And the way that you've been
feeling and the weight that you've been carrying is
going to be much easier to shift than you realise.*

*The answer lies with your mindset, the set of thoughts
you hold about yourself and your life.*

*Get ready for life to feel lighter and easier for you, because when
you get your mindset right, everything else falls into place.*

CONTENTS

A NOTE FROM DOMONIQUE ...

I was first introduced to the idea of a detox (although this was a dietary one) about twenty years ago when I was trying to address an uncomfortable digestive complaint. I went to see a rather strict woman known around London as the Detox Queen, and under her supervision my regime involved giving up all the usual suspects: alcohol, sugar, caffeine, gluten and dairy.

I'm not going to lie to you, those first few days were not my favourite days. I felt like I had a hangover, even though I hadn't had a drink, and I found myself thinking about chocolate when I woke up, when I went to bed and pretty much every minute in between.

But after the first few days, I started to notice a change. My head became clearer, my body felt lighter and more energised, and my stomach once again felt like it belonged to me, not something that had been invaded by body snatchers!

What I also came to realise, as I kicked my unhealthy habits to the kerb, was that the things I thought I had been eating in moderation or only occasionally had actually become more of a daily fix. I realised that my days were actually *filled* with unhealthy habits. And now that I was free of those habits, I really did feel like a brand-new person.

And this is what I want *9 Step Negativity Detox* to do for you.

Right now, your mindset isn't always working for you; in fact, sometimes it's actually working against you. But with this book, we're going to change all that. I'm going to show you how to detox your mindset and eliminate negativity from your life so that your life will feel lighter and easier for you. Once you are free and clear of the unnecessary causes of negativity in your life, not only will you discover how pervasive your negative thoughts and experiences have really been, but you'll be much better able to spot them and prevent them from creeping back into your life.

And the good news – you can still eat chocolate if you want to!

Just like the detox I went on all those years ago, some of the things you'll learn here or the ideas I'll share might make you a little uncomfortable. It might make you think about things in ways you're not used to or encourage you to face up to certain challenges once and for all. When this happens, please don't tune out or press fast forward.

Instead, sit with your feelings and see what you can learn from them – what insights or lessons do they hold?

~~~

You need to get comfortable with discomfort if
you want to live your best, most brilliant life.

Most people are fine with 'fine' and okay with their life being just 'okay', but if you want to live a happy and fulfilling life, it's important that you're not. But you've chosen to read this book, so I don't think I need to remind you of that. I'm guessing that you're here because you're already fully committed to doing whatever you need to do to live your best, most brilliant life.

Let's get started …

WELCOME TO THE 9 STEPS

STEP 1: SELECT YOUR VIEW

To begin, I'll show you how to choose what you want to focus your attention on and how you want to experience your life. You'll learn how to put on your rose-coloured glasses and discover the power of a positive perspective, and by the end of this chapter you'll be able to train that perspective on yourself.

STEP 2: FILL YOUR CUP

Learn how to increase your awareness of the abundance in your life. By the end of this chapter, instead of worrying about what you don't have or feeling like your glass is half empty, you'll know how to express your gratitude and to be grateful that you have a glass to fill.

STEP 3: FIND YOUR PEOPLE

Not everyone you meet will be your kind of person. In this step you'll find ways to work out who you want to spend your time with and why friendships sometimes change. By the end of this chapter you'll have a clear understanding of what you want and need from your friendships and how to easily spot your kindreds in a crowd.

STEP 4: EXPAND YOUR MIND

Learn how to open your mind, let go of unhelpful and outdated thoughts and develop new ones that serve you instead. By the end of this chapter not only will you have identified the limiting beliefs and behaviours you never knew you had, you'll be well on your way to liberating yourself from them.

STEP 5: LOVE YOUR BODY

In this chapter we'll look at the way you feel about your body. Your body may not be perfect but instead of focusing on everything it's not, I'm going to teach you how to treat it with respect and appreciate it for all that it is. You'll learn to see your body in a whole new light and have a much healthier relationship with it.

STEP 6: PICK YOUR BATTLES

Every life has its highs and lows, but that doesn't mean that you have to turn the down times into an uphill battle. I'll teach you to focus on what you *can* influence and not to fight things that are outside of your control. By the end of this chapter you'll know how to be assertive when you want to and how to take a deep breath and let it go when you need to.

STEP 7: CHOOSE YOUR FAMILY

While you may not be able to choose the family of your childhood, as an adult you get to decide which relationships you want to invest in and which ones you're happy to let drift away.

By the end of this chapter not only will you understand why your relationship with your parents is so complicated, you'll be crystal clear on what it really means to be a grown-up.

STEP 8: BE YOUR BOSS

It's only when you learn how to take charge and focus on what you really want from life that you can actually start to get it. You deserve to be living a happy and fulfilling life and by the end of this chapter you'll know exactly what you need to do to get it.

STEP 9: CELEBRATE YOUR SELF

I'm going to show you how to break the cycle of endless self-criticism, how to lift yourself up when you're feeling down, and how to always see the best in yourself. By the end of this chapter you'll know how to stop playing small, hiding your light and being anything less than all that you have the potential to be.

As you read each chapter, I'd love to know what your biggest insights and your favourite mindset shifts have been. You can find me on Instagram or Facebook at domoniquebertolucci – I can't wait to hear your thoughts. And while you're over on social media why not share a pic of whatever it is you're doing while you're reading this book – tag me, tag @hardiegrantbooks and tag a friend who you think would enjoy it too. Use the hashtag #negativitydetox so I can keep an eye out for you and cheer you along.

Throughout this book, I'll be sharing a whole range of tips, strategies and suggestions so you can shift the sources of negativity from your life. To help you put everything you're learning into action, I've created a workbook that has some extra exercises and expanded journal prompts. I've also included some bonus resources that I just couldn't fit into this book.

The workbook is free, and you can download it from domoniquebertolucci.com/negativity-detox.

SELECT YOUR VIEW

Decide what you want to focus your attention on and how you want to experience your life.

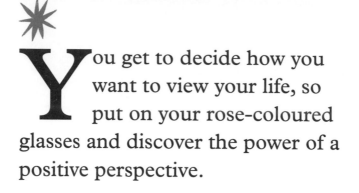

You get to decide how you want to view your life, so put on your rose-coloured glasses and discover the power of a positive perspective.

I was first introduced to the idea that you could create your own reality way back when I was twenty. I had just moved out of home, across the country and towards what would be the first of many life-changing experiences. A book I was reading presented the idea of creating your own reality as a mix of quantum and metaphysical concepts – the time/space continuum, are we really here, and is anything real anyway? You know the kind.

While I found those ideas interesting (and challenging) I realised that I had access to a much more practical and everyday way to create my reality – I could simply decide what I was, and wasn't, going to pay attention to in my life.

Over the years I've taught myself to tune out sounds I don't want to hear, and I know I'd be a terrible eyewitness because when I look around me, my eye only catches things that I find appealing and filters out everything else. I've also learned to see my life experiences in the best possible light and not to hold too tightly to things that are unpleasant or upsetting to me.

My life has had ups and downs just like everyone else; I was subjected to horrendous bullying as a child and then again at the hands of a sociopathic boss. My heart has been broken. I've been left black and blue by a car accident that nearly killed me, and I miscarried more times than I like to count before I was able to conceive my son.

My list of ups and downs, just like everyone else's, goes on. But I knew that I had mastered the art of creating my reality when I was attending a seminar and the speaker asked us to cast our mind back to an upsetting experience that had occurred in the past year … and I couldn't think of one. Not. A. Single. One. Of course, later that day a number of experiences that hadn't been so great came to mind – but at the time, I couldn't recall one. All I could think was that on balance, my life was pretty good.

✳ ✳ ✳

✳ CHOOSE A POSITIVE ✳
PERSPECTIVE

The first thing you need to do if you want to detox your mindset and eliminate negativity from your life is to choose a positive perspective. When you have a positive perspective, you can see the best in each situation you experience, each person you encounter and even in yourself.

How you view the experiences in your life – the comings and goings, ups and downs, victories and failures – will directly influence how you process these encounters in your life. If that sounds like a crazy Catch-22 or some sort of word puzzle, let's examine that powerful reframe another way. Although you can't change what happens in your life, you can change the way you think about what happens *and that* will change the way you feel about it.

〜〜

Choosing a positive perspective doesn't mean that negative things won't happen, but it does mean that you won't mind nearly so much when they do.

In *7 Step Mindset Makeover* I wrote about a process I call the Architecture of Change: a three-part approach to creating lasting and lifelong change in your life.

Just as an architect will create a 3D plan to understand how a finished project will look, the Architecture of Change teaches you to consider three separate aspects if you want to get to any desired end result – your Head Space, your Heart Space and your Dynamic Space. These three 'spaces of change' need to be considered together and not separately if you want to achieve your goals, create new habits and make lasting change something you can do with ease.

But understanding the Architecture of Change won't just help you to make changes in your life, it will also help you to change the way you *feel* about your life. Instead of automatically letting your feelings control the way you feel about something that is happening, when you choose a positive perspective you are actively choosing your Head Space and consciously deciding how you want to think about your given situation. This in turn will influence your Heart Space – how you feel about the situation. When you actively choose a positive perspective, you automatically dim your view of the negative perspective and any negative or unwelcome feelings will be dimmed along with it.

I tell my clients that changing your thoughts is the starting point of any life change: change your thoughts, change your feelings, change your life – and it really can be as simple as that. By choosing a positive perspective, even if the situation is far from perfect, you will have a much more positive experience.

Choosing a positive perspective doesn't mean you should turn a blind eye to the negative consequences of a situation or that you should be naively optimistic. Instead, I like to think of it like one of those tourist viewfinders you see at landmarks and lookouts. You know the kind – they cost a dollar to use and they're like a pair of binoculars on a stand. You can rotate them a full 360 degrees and then when you see something that interests you, you can zoom right in.

Choosing your perspective is about choosing which part of your picture you want to focus on.

STOP WORRYING

When you worry, you are thinking about something that might happen – a potentially negative experience that may, or may not, occur. But no matter how much energy you put into your worries you will never change the outcome.

~~~

Worrying won't change anything except your ability to enjoy your life and to be truly present in it.

If you want something to go well or turn out for the best, it's not a bad idea to consider, and understand, all the ways it could go wrong. But this line of thinking should be treated as a risk assessment and not the main focus for your thoughts. Think of it in much the same way as you would when you take out an insurance policy. Whether it is for your home, your car or a trip, you're investing in your policy in the hope that you never actually need to use it.

Once you know what the risks are, and what you would do if they became a reality, it's time to park that knowledge and spend the rest of your time and energy doing whatever you can do to support the outcome you really want.

✳ FOCUS YOUR ATTENTION ✳ ON YOUR INTENTION

If you want things to turn out well in your life, this needs to be the outcome you focus on and where the majority of your attention needs to go. But to be able to focus on your intention you need to have a clear idea of what that intention actually is. I see far too many people moving through life worrying about what might happen, instead of confidently taking the steps they need to take to make the things they really do want to happen, happen.

Many people never develop more than a vague idea about what they want. They don't stop to think deeply about what they really want and what really matters in their life – and then they drift along wondering why they never get it.

In order to get clear on your intentions you need to ask yourself, 'What do I want to say and how do I want to feel about who I am and the life I live?' It is your answer to these questions that will act as your compass and help you move your life in the direction you want it to go in.

*Get clear on your intentions and focus
your attention on them.*

When you focus your attention on your intention, you are directing your energy towards what you want, rather than wasting it by thinking about what you don't want, or worse, simply letting what you *do* want fade away.

✳ LOOK FOR POSITIVE OPPORTUNITIES ✳ IN EVERY EXPERIENCE

If you're committed to living a full and interesting life, a whole range of experiences are going to come your way. While I'd love to be able to promise you that simply by choosing a positive perspective, each and every one of those experiences will be a happy one, you and I both know that is unlikely to be the case. But even when life throws things at you that you would toss away if only you could, you still get to choose how you want to experience them by looking for the opportunity the experience has created for you.

You get to choose how you experience your life.

If a friend cancels your plans at the last minute, you can instead enjoy an evening of 'me time'. If it rains when you were planning a picnic, you can spend the afternoon playing board games or watching a movie marathon, and if you didn't get the job you were going for, you can remind yourself that the interview was good practice for the dream job that will eventually come your way.

Of course, it is much easier to choose a positive perspective when the things that aren't going right in your life are pretty straightforward and the consequences aren't that severe. It's a lot harder when the situation is more serious or when the stakes are higher.

I am not a fan of the expression 'everything happens for a reason'. While it might look cute on a fridge magnet, I believe it is a trite expression that brings no comfort to anyone who is experiencing serious misfortune, heartbreak or tragedy. Yes, these things have occurred for a 'reason', but that reason is factual or scientific. If you've been made redundant or laid off at work, the reason is that your company could no longer afford to pay you or justify having someone in your role. When someone dies of cancer, the reason is that the disease was stronger than the treatment. When a marriage ends because of an infidelity, the reason is that the betrayal was deemed unforgivable.

I don't believe that everything happens for a reason, but I do believe that we each have the opportunity to find our own reason and meaning in the things that happen.

✳ SEE THINGS ✳ COMPASSIONATELY

It can be extremely frustrating when things don't go your way through no fault of your own, and it's even worse when it feels like someone else is to blame, but if you're committed to eliminating negativity from your life, you need to choose to see things compassionately. The truth is that most people are doing their best most of the time. Someone else's 'best' might not be up to your standards – it might be compromised by something else going on in their life or it might still be in its development stage. Whatever the reason it's unlikely that they were intentionally trying to make you angry or cause you stress in any way.

〰

Most people are doing their best most of the time.

When you find yourself in a situation like this it can be easy to rant and rave – but it's rarely worth it. Whether your anger is outwardly expressed or bottled up inside, the only person it is really hurting is you. Instead of raging with frustration, make the decision to be compassionate. When you accept that most people are doing their best most of the time, it becomes much easier to practise forgiveness and find the acceptance you need, to exhale and let the whole negative experience pass on by.

✳ *STOP FOCUSING ON PEOPLE'S FAULTS ...* ✳
YOURS AS WELL AS EVERYONE ELSE'S

It can be easy to spend your time criticising other people, especially as a distraction from criticising yourself, but if you want to eliminate negativity from your life, you need to stop focusing on people's faults – yours as well as everyone else's. Nobody is perfect, but you can waste a lot of energy and create a lot of negativity by focusing your attention on other people's imperfections: the things you wish they would do differently, the flaws in their character and the way they are getting things wrong in their life.

~~~

When it comes to being human, there's
no one right way to do it.

Whether it's trying to be a good parent, friend, sibling, partner, employer or colleague, your way won't be the only way. And there's no one right way to manage your money, build your career, choose a partner or meet any of the other challenges life throws at you. Everyone will have their own approach and while the path that some people take will instantly resonate with you, others will seem completely off the mark.

One of my favourite quotes is from the French writer Voltaire who said, 'Judge a person by their questions, rather than by their answers'.

We are all trying to get it right – 'it' being this thing called life! Everyone has different values and no one value is more valuable than another. When you find yourself judging someone's choices what you are really doing is judging them for having different values to yours.

This idea is never clearer to me than when I look at all the different ways my friends and extended family choose to parent their children. I used to find myself feeling frustrated, and I'll confess to having wasted time internally criticising and complaining about the things other people were doing – especially when it came to things like routines, discipline and all the other hot topics for people with young children.

I had a realisation one day that changed everything and eliminated all the negativity that this had been bringing into my life. I realised that the people whose choices were frustrating me loved their children just as much as I loved mine. That while we each had different approaches to the details of how we parented, we were all trying to achieve the same end result: to raise happy, healthy, well-loved children. The details of how people did things differently stopped bothering me, because I realised that was all they were – details. The outcome we were all trying to achieve was exactly the same.

Instead of wasting precious energy and engaging in the negativity of what is essentially a version of 'my way or the highway', remind yourself that, as adults, we are all free to live our lives in accordance with our own unique set of values. Rather than criticising others for theirs, refocus your energy on honouring yours.

✳ LEAVE GOSSIP ✳
AT THE DOOR

Eleanor Roosevelt once said, 'Great minds discuss ideas, average minds discuss events, small minds discuss people'. Every time you gossip, regardless of whether you are gossiping about someone you know or a celebrity you've read about online, you are actively welcoming negativity into your life.

~~~

Finding entertainment in other people's
misfortune is never healthy.

At the time, and in the moment, focusing on someone else's mistakes and missteps can feel like entertainment, especially when it offers a welcome distraction from the highs and lows you might be experiencing in your own life, but finding entertainment in other people's misfortune is never healthy. While you might enjoy the short-term high that comes from thinking, 'Well, it's not all bad – at least my life doesn't look like that!', this negativity will only ever give your self-esteem a false boost, one that is bound to expire the next time something that makes you feel inadequate comes along.

✳ ACCEPT THAT YOU'RE GOING ✳ TO MAKE MISTAKES

Now that you've elevated your mindset above the negativity that is generated whenever you engage in gossip or sit in judgement about other people's mistakes, it's time to accept that you are going to make mistakes too.

〜〜

*No matter how hard you try, you are
not going to get everything right.*

You are going to mess up, get things wrong, hurt someone's feelings or let someone down in some way. When this happens, instead of berating yourself and dragging yourself down with a barrage of negativity and self-criticism – forgive yourself.

Accept that mistakes happen, and then look at what you can learn from this experience, so that you can make sure that this particular mistake never happens again.

✳ ✳ ✳

✳ FOCUS ON YOUR ✳
STRENGTHS

When it comes to having a positive perspective, there really isn't a more important place to cast your rose-coloured gaze than at yourself.

It's easy to fall into the habit of constantly criticising yourself or comparing yourself to others and routinely finding that you come up short. But instead of running the list of things that are wrong with you on an endless loop in your head, make the decision to accept any flaws you have, and shift your focus to all of your strengths instead.

You might not be perfect – we both know perfection is an unattainable goal anyway! – but the very fact that you have chosen to read this book tells me that you are someone who *wants* to be the best they can be, and someone who is *committed* to living their best and most brilliant life.

〜〜

You might not be perfect, but there's
a lot that is good about you.

Take the time to make a list of your strengths, positive qualities, successes and achievements. Although you might want to start thinking about your list right away, this is not intended to be just a mental exercise. I want you to write down all the things that are great about you, your positive qualities, things you've done well and things you feel proud of and then continue to add to it over time.

Once you have your list, I want you to keep it close by – your wallet, bedside table or even on your phone. Somewhere you can quickly find it and refer back to it whenever you are having a down day, could do with a boost and need help nudging your negativity out the door.

KATE'S NEGATIVITY DETOX

Step 1 was a bit of a wake-up call for me. I've always been a perfectionist, and to be honest, until now, I've been telling myself that is a good thing. I've got high standards at work, I expect people to do their jobs properly, and I try to make sure my children have good manners. But now I realise that, while I think I like the standards I have for myself, I'm often quite judgemental and critical of anyone around me if I think they don't measure up ... and that's not a particularly nice way to be.

I realise now that part of the pressure I place on myself to get everything done perfectly is because I've been worrying about what will go wrong if I don't. I know I'm respected at work, so I'm probably not going to get fired if I make a simple mistake; and if I leave the house without it being immaculate, is the world going to end? No. I can see now the level of pressure I've been placing on everything.

I've been judging everyone else for their mistakes or failings while worrying everyone is going to judge me for mine. This step has helped me to see that this whole approach is creating a lot of unnecessary stress and tension in my life and that I have a choice about how I view things.

From now on, I'm going to take my favourite lesson from Step 1 and accept that most people are doing their best most of the time ... even me!

KEY
INSIGHTS

STEP 1: SELECT YOUR VIEW

1. Choose a positive perspective and see the best in every situation.
2. Stop worrying. Worry won't change anything – ever.
3. Focus your attention on your intention and focus your energy on making that intention your reality.
4. Look for the opportunity that every situation holds – while you can't change what happens, you can change how you experience it.
5. Remember, most people are doing their best most of the time.
6. No one value is more valuable than another, so stop criticising people for having different values to yours.
7. Don't gossip – entertaining yourself with someone's mistakes and missteps will never feel good for long.
8. Accept that mistakes happen – learn from them so you don't make the same mistakes twice.
9. Make a list of your strengths, and keep your list close to hand – and to heart.

JOURNAL PROMPTS

1. Think about something you have been worrying about. Instead of worrying, is there an action you could be taking or a shift in perspective you should be making?

2. Think about a time when someone disappointed you or let you down. Knowing that most people are doing their best most of the time, how might you reframe this experience?

3. Make a list of your strengths, positive qualities and personal achievements. Don't limit your list just to big things; the goal here is to create a long list, so include as many things as you can think of.

STEP 2

FILL YOUR CUP

Stop worrying about what you don't have or feeling like your glass is half empty – just be grateful that you have a glass to fill.

When you acknowledge all the abundance in your life, you will discover that you have so much more to feel grateful for than you ever realised before.

At least once a week at our house, we go around the dinner table and share three things that have brought us joy over the course of the last week and three things that we are feeling grateful for. I admit, sometimes when I say it's time for joy and gratitude, my family moan about it and complain that living with a life coach can be a bit tough! But as we go around the table, I notice two things: firstly, as each person shares the things that gave them joy or that they are grateful for, other family members' lists grow too, as things they might not have noticed or hadn't thought to acknowledge get highlighted by the person whose turn it is to share.

The second thing I notice is that even if we are all already in a good mood, the energy around the table gets lighter as people throw off their concerns of the day and focus on all that is good about their lives. Invariably, later on that evening, one of my children or my husband will come to me and want to share more about why they are feeling good about those positive things.

By articulating our gratitude and sharing it with each other, it's as if our own feelings of gratitude have grown, and by training our minds to seek out joy we are able to welcome even more of it into our lives.

✳ ✳ ✳

✷ DEVELOP AN ATTITUDE ✷ OF GRATITUDE

It's widely documented that acknowledging gratitude is a tonic for your mental health. Countless researchers have found that focusing on gratitude – the things you are grateful for – is a huge benefit to our mental and emotional wellbeing and that regularly practising gratitude leads us to feel good about ourselves and our lives.

But despite this, I often hear people talking about the things that are missing from their life – the things they can't afford, things that haven't happened and places they haven't been – instead of focusing on all that they do have.

~~~

Express your gratitude each and every day.

Nightly prayers were once commonplace in our society. Invariably prayers would include an opportunity for thanks – 'and thank you for … ' – which was an acknowledgement of gratitude. While I don't believe you need to be religious to be happy, I firmly believe that this habit of expressing your gratitude each day, whether to God, the universe or simply to yourself, is one that everyone can benefit from.

✴ KEEP A ✴ GRATITUDE LIST

In order to express your gratitude, you need to have things to be grateful for; and although your life might be filled with them, if you're not paying attention they can easily pass you by. As well as creating the daily, or at least regular, habit of reflecting on all that you have to be grateful for, I want you to keep a gratitude list or journal.

~~~

Documenting the things you are grateful for expands the powerful effect gratitude has on your sense of happiness and fulfilment in your life.

It's much easier to think about all the things that are good about your life when everything is going well, but it's when you're going through a tough time or experiencing a slump that your gratitude list will really come into its own. Whenever you find yourself feeling low or disappointed with some aspect of your life, you will be able to take out your list of all the things that are still good about your life and balance your current negative perspective or experience with a more accurate view of your life.

✳ UNDERSTAND THE DIFFERENCE ✳ BETWEEN WANTS AND NEEDS

It's been a long time since I was an undergraduate, but it is no surprise to me that the topic I remember most clearly was Maslow and the hierarchy of needs.

You too might have heard of Abraham Maslow and his pyramid that reached from our most basic physiological needs – food, water, shelter – all the way through to self-actualisation, the desire to fulfil your potential in life. The thinking behind the model is that people are only motivated by the desire for the next category of items or 'needs' when the preceding set of needs are met. For example, people are only driven by prestige or self-esteem when they have their physiological, safety, love and belonging needs met.

As a student, this was an eye-opener as to what drives people. As a coach, it reminds me where people are so often going wrong.

The majority of people I speak to have all of their needs met in those first few critical levels. They have all the food they need, access to clean water and a safe and secure home, and they have a range of people in their lives who care deeply about them. It makes sense then, just as Maslow explained, that the next thing they would be seeking would be their esteem needs: the need for prestige and accomplishment. The only problem is that somewhere along the way, people have confused 'need', which in Maslow's context means 'driver for motivation', with a real and genuine requirement.

I need a new car, I need a bigger house, I need an overseas holiday, I need a pay rise, I need … I need … I need.

Don't get me wrong, all those desires sound valid to me, but that is exactly what they are – desires. They are wants, not needs in any true sense of the word.

~~~

Although there may be things that you want, the
majority of your needs have already been met.

If you want to experience more gratitude and have a greater sense of abundance in your life, you need to get clear about the difference between your wants and your needs. The easiest way to do this is to focus on your gratitude for all that you already have. It's only when you focus on how abundant your life already is that you can see, quite clearly, that the majority of the things that are missing or not yet present are things you want or desire – they are wants, not needs.

✳ ✳ ✳

✹ FOCUS ON THE WEALTH AND ABUNDANCE ✹ ALREADY IN YOUR LIFE

Crying poor and focusing on what you don't have is a very unhelpful mindset habit – one that will stop you from enjoying the wealth and abundance in your life. I regularly hear people complain about not being able to afford a home extension, or to send their children to the right school or buy the latest must-have gadget, all the while having more than enough food on the table, a roof over their head, clothes in their wardrobe and, in most cases, money in the bank.

The level of material abundance in the majority of people's lives means they shouldn't have anything to complain about, but unfortunately, in the consumption-crazy times we live in, there are a lot of very comfortable people who are convinced they don't have enough.

Be grateful for all that you already have.

Even though there might be other or additional things you desire, you can still enjoy the things you already have. These are not mutually exclusive settings. Enjoying the roof over your head doesn't stop you from planning to buy a bigger house, any more than enjoying a cheap and cheerful holiday prevents you from saving up for something more expensive next time.

Being grateful for all that you *already* have in life won't hold you back from having more – it will just mean that you enjoy the life you have right now so much more.

✳ TRACK YOUR ✳ GOOD FORTUNE

A really great way to increase your appreciation of the wealth and abundance in your life is to routinely track it – to actually write it down. But instead of just writing down your income or the value of your car or home – standard items for any wealth assessment – I want you to make a note of the things that have been gifted to you, that you received but didn't have to pay for or which you bought at a discount.

For example, if a friend pays for your coffee, note down the price of the coffee; if you are given a book you were planning to buy, write down the value of the book; and if a pre-planned purchase was discounted by the time you actually bought it, make a note of the amount that you saved.

〰

Life is filled with unexpected gifts – make sure to acknowledge yours.

Becoming aware of all the wealth and abundance in your life will increase your sense of gratitude for all that you have, and you may soon find yourself wondering if you're going to need a bigger cup!

✳ STOP COMPARING YOUR ✳ WEALTH TO OTHERS'

Now that you're getting better at recognising all the wealth in *your* life, it's time to stop paying so much attention to the wealth in *everyone else's* life. When you start directly comparing your position, and what you do or don't have, it's easy to fall into the trap of thinking that everybody else has much more than you.

Maybe they do. Maybe they don't.

Whatever anyone else does or doesn't have in their life shouldn't impact the way you feel about your life.

Everyone makes different choices, prioritises different things and honours different values. Those choices, priorities and values will shape your individual path and impact your bank balance, career progress and other external measures of success.

Instead of comparing your life against other people's and coming up short, measure your life by how aligned it is to your values.

✳ ✳ ✳

✳ BE ✳
GENEROUS

One of the easiest ways to fill your cup and expand the feeling of gratitude and abundance in your life is to be generous. While it might sound counterintuitive, when you are generous, whether it is with your time, money or energy, your awareness of your ability to give shifts to the front of your mind. Whether it's supporting your local community, contributing to a charity or non-profit, or volunteering to help those less fortunate than yourself, giving of yourself in this way reminds you of how fortunate you are.

If you want to feel abundant, look at all the ways you can give and give back.

When you are feeling poor, make a donation. If you are feeling overwhelmed, offer to help someone out in whatever small way you can, and if you find yourself feeling like life is getting the better of you, have a look beyond your own situation and see how you can make life better for someone else.

✳✳✳

✳ APPRECIATE YOUR LIFE ✳
FOR ALL THAT IT IS

Nobody's life follows a straight line to happiness and success. I'm always joking with my friends that it has taken me the best part of twenty years to become an overnight success – except that, like all the best jokes, it really is quite close to the truth.

Regardless of where your life is at right now, there is bound to be some good in it. It's time to start paying better attention to your life so you can properly appreciate it.

Every time you experience a victory or something goes well in your life it is easy to see how you might feel grateful for it. But even when things aren't running smoothly, and life feels hard, there is always still something to be grateful for.

When life feels tough, challenge yourself to feel grateful for the lesson you are learning. I say 'challenge' because it isn't always the easiest thing to do. It is easy to feel sorry for yourself, but when you focus on what you have learned even the most negative experiences will still provide you with something positive.

Every experience holds a lesson and while learning it might be painful at the time, your life will end up being richer for it.

When you feel like you're in a slump or like nothing is going your way, it's even more important to focus on your gratitude. And if you can't find anything to feel good about in that moment, you'll be glad for that list I encouraged you to make back when you were feeling great.

✳ WORK ON YOUR ✳ GRATITUDE 'MUSCLE'

If you feel weird or awkward expressing your gratitude, even just to yourself, remind yourself that acknowledging gratitude is just like anything else – it will get easier and you will get better at it with practice. Whether you keep a gratitude journal, speak your gratitude out loud like we do at our family dinner, or jot your daily gratitude down on a planner like the Brilliant Day Planner I created for my clients, the more you do it the better you'll get and the more you will get out of it.

Keep your gratitude at the top of your mind.

If it's hard to think of the things you're feeling grateful for, it doesn't mean you don't have anything to be grateful for, it just means that your gratitude has been too far from your mind.

If you're not sure where to begin, make sure you download the free workbook that goes with this book. It includes a link to download a free copy of my Brilliant Day Planner so you can start practising daily gratitude right away. You can get it at domoniquebertolucci.com/negativity-detox.

✳✳✳

DAVID'S NEGATIVITY DETOX

I've always been ambitious … even as a kid I was always working on one scheme or another that was going to make me rich. Over the years I've built several successful businesses, but I've also had some big disappointments; a property development that barely broke even is a particularly painful example.

When I started thinking about this step and filling my cup, I thought, 'Yeah, I get this already – I love my kids and I appreciate my health', but it was only as I went a bit deeper that I realised the 'poverty mentality' that I've been carrying around with me.

I know I've been successful, but I'm not even close to the level of success the people I admire have reached – billionaires like Richard Branson, Jeff Bezos and Elon Musk – and I can't really see me ever getting there. I'm not in the same league; I'm not even in their sport!

This step made me realise that this attitude has left me with my own version of a poverty mentality. I've made lots of money over the years, but I never allow myself to feel properly wealthy or to enjoy it. I might enjoy some of the trappings of it, like buying a new car, but I've realised that I never feel rich or successful inside.

I think that, on some subconscious level, I believed that if I let myself feel successful, I'd start resting on my laurels or become complacent about my goals.

I've been so focused on what I want to do next and how far I still have to go that I haven't been appreciating the successes I've had and the things I have achieved. Thinking about how I fill my cup has made me want to change that. From now on, I'm going to pay attention to my gratitude for the things I do have and acknowledge the success I have achieved.

KEY
INSIGHTS

STEP 2: FILL YOUR CUP

1. Develop an attitude of gratitude. Make acknowledging and articulating your gratitude a priority in your life.
2. Keep a gratitude list. Make a note of all the things you have to feel grateful for, and refer to it any time you feel like you need a boost.
3. Get clear on the difference between your wants and your needs, and recognise how many of your needs have already been met.
4. Ditch the poverty mentality – you are much richer than you think.
5. Keep a record of all the good fortune that comes your way, and watch how it adds up over time.
6. Don't compare yourself or your position in life to anyone else's – ever.
7. The fastest way to feel your life is abundant is to be generous – give back and give often.
8. Appreciate your life for all that it already is.
9. Work on your gratitude 'muscle' – the more you express your gratitude the better at it you'll become.

JOURNAL PROMPTS

1. Make a list of three things you are grateful for in three
    different areas of your life.

2. Looking back over the past month, make a list of all the
    times you experienced good fortune. For example, a friend
    buys you coffee, or if something you wanted to buy is
    discounted or goes on sale.

3. Describe your life as it might appear to someone who doesn't
    know you and is looking at it from the outside. Focus your
    attention on all the good fortune, wealth and abundance in
    your life.

FIND YOUR PEOPLE

Be clear about who you want
to spend your time with and
what you need in order for your
friendships to thrive.

Your true friends will accept your imperfections and love you for the person that you are. When you know what you are looking for in a friendship, it will be easy to spot your kindreds in a crowd.

Not so long ago, I was chatting with someone about a group of my oldest and dearest friends – some of us met in primary school, others in high school. The average duration of the friendships within this particular circle is thirty-five years!

The person I was talking to commented that it was unusual to still be such close friends with people from our schooldays and how remarkable it was that we hadn't grown apart or drifted away from each other over the years.

But as I explained, the real reason we are all still such close friends is actually the opposite.

It is not that we've never drifted apart, it's that our individual life journeys have meant that we have had to choose each other again and again.

Between us, we have lived in nearly every capital city in Australia, and at various times one or more of us has lived outside of Australia: in North America, South America, Europe and Asia. Sometimes one person's physical absences have lasted a year or two, a posting for work here or a transfer there. Other absences have lasted much, much longer. In fact, thanks to my two long stints in London, it has been more than thirty years since we all lived in the same city at the same time.

The friendships within this circle are beyond strong.

I know each one of my friends would walk on hot coals for me or any one of the others. And I would do the same for them. Our friendship is strong, not because some of us went to high school together – there are lots of lovely people from my high school days that I've long lost touch with – but because we've consciously chosen each other individually, and collectively, again and again.

✸ CONSCIOUSLY CHOOSE ✸ YOUR FRIENDS

The first thing you need to do if you want to have deep and satisfying friendships is to consciously choose your friends.

Your friendships are an investment.

Your friendships are an investment – creating quality friendships takes time and energy – so like any investment, you need to make wise choices about where to direct your resources.

✳ ✳ ✳

✳ ACCEPT THAT FRIENDSHIPS ✳ CHANGE

So many friendships form out of circumstance – your classmates, colleagues, teammates and so on – but not everybody you spend time with deserves a place on your friendship 'A' list. And even if they were on that list at one point, it doesn't mean that they deserve to stay there forever.

'Here for a reason, here for a season, here for a lifetime.'

The first time I heard this expression, it made so much about the ebb and flow of various friendships over the years make more sense to me.

From the intense friendships of your teenage years, to bonds formed over horrible bosses; whether it's those who share a milestone with you, like the birth of your first child; or the people who hang out at the same school gates or on the sidelines of a playing field – the majority of your friendships will run their natural course.

~~~

Not every friendship you make is going to last a lifetime, nor is it supposed to.

You might move suburbs or change companies. You might lose interest in something that was once fascinating, move through a phase of life, or simply decide that you no longer have enough spare time to fit a particular relationship in. Instead of feeling guilty about not keeping in touch with people or feeling obliged to spend time with people who no longer light you up, make a conscious decision about which friendships you want to invest in and which relationships you are happy to let drift away.

The majority of the time two people's expectations of a friendship will be evenly matched but every now and then you might be the one who is assigned to the 'B' list. When this happens, it can feel really hurtful. Perhaps you've made an effort and it hasn't been reciprocated, or maybe you feel like you've been replaced. Instead of agonising over what went wrong, whether on your side or theirs, acknowledge your hurt and then accept that not all friendships last forever; that either the reason for this friendship has expired or that the season for this friendship has simply passed.

Mentally wish your friend well and then shift their name down to acquaintance on your list.

✳ ✳ ✳

✹ GET CLEAR ABOUT ✹ YOUR VALUES

Your values are the things that matter most to you – your non-negotiables in life. As well as knowing what the values are for your whole life, you also need to know them for each important area of your life, and this includes understanding what you value in a friendship.

Look around you, at the people you spend the majority of your time with. Chances are that while you feel a deep connection to some, others are simply people with whom you spend your time. When we say someone is 'on the same wavelength' as us, what we mean is that the person thinks and feels in a similar way to us – and what that means is that we share common or compatible values. And those people that you just don't gel with? You guessed it, it's more than just a lack of common interest, it's usually because your values are misaligned.

~~~

Focus on building friendships with people whose values are compatible with yours.

The people you choose as friends don't need to have identical values to yours, but their values need to be compatible rather than in conflict with yours. If you find yourself feeling frequently frustrated or let down by a friend, it's probably because you have different values about whatever it is that's causing the conflict. Instead of speaking badly about someone or criticising them behind their back, take the time to work out why their behaviour is bothering you and to understand which of your values it is jarring with.

Creating and maintaining friendships takes time and energy, so you want to make sure you are expending yours wisely. When you know what your values are, it will be much easier to tell who has the potential to be a good friend and who should remain someone you are simply friendly with.

✳ BE CLEAR ABOUT ✳ YOUR TERMS

Every relationship – social, romantic, professional or familial – is governed by a set of terms and conditions. These may be spoken or unspoken, explicit or assumed: forsaking all others, don't be late for dinner, or do what you say you're going to do when you say you're going to do it.

Friendships are no different, and whether you have stopped to consider it or not, every one of your friendships has a set of terms and acceptable conditions it is operating under. While you might not have ever signed a contract, your closest friends – the people you trust implicitly and with whom you just click – will not only have values that are compatible with yours, but they will be conducting the friendship under a similar set of terms.

~~~

Reflect on how you think friends should treat each other and only invest your energy in friendships with people who feel the same.

A few years ago, when my daughter was in primary school, she experienced a recurring conflict with a frenemy: someone who said she was a friend but behaved in a way that was anything but.

When I talked to my daughter about this relationship, I asked her to consider what she wanted from a friendship and how she thought friends should behave towards each other. After she'd had time to reflect, I asked her if this girl was the kind of person she wanted for a friend. This simple enquiry gave my daughter all the clarity needed to see that while she could continue to behave in a friendly manner when she needed to interact with this girl, she would no longer consider her a friend.

Whether you are aged nine or ninety-nine, my advice for navigating your relationships is the same – look for people who share the same ideas about what a good relationship is.

✳ AUDIT YOUR ✳ ADDRESS BOOK

If you find there are people in your life that bring more negativity than positivity with them, consider how much time you currently spend with them and if you need to cut back or perhaps remove yourself from the relationship altogether. People are often uncomfortable when I bring this idea up. They question if it is mean or unkind not to want to pursue a friendship with someone. But if you want to live a happy and fulfilling life, you need to make conscious choices and that applies to your friendships and social life too.

If you find that you don't enjoy someone's company – perhaps you feel criticised or put down by them, disrespected or offended by their idea of humour, or find that their values are simply not compatible with yours – remind yourself that you are under no obligation to continue to be in their company.

〜〜

It's time to stop wasting your precious energy
resisting other people's negativity.

You don't need to lie or make up excuses to turn down an unwanted invitation. You can simply say, 'Thank you, but I have other plans', even if those plans are to sit at home with a good book.

I'm not talking about ghosting someone or ignoring them altogether. But you really don't have to return that invitation to dinner, set up another coffee catch-up, go on another date or arrange another playdate for your children if you feel dragged down when you are in their company. This is not about being nice versus being rude. Or kind versus unkind. This is about deciding how you want to spend your time and who you want to spend it with.

✳ ✳ ✳

✳ MONITOR YOUR ✳ REACTIONS

Just as you don't have to accept the negativity brought into your life by people you don't care about, there are ways to manage when the source of the negativity is someone you really do like and care about.

Sometimes it's a relationship that you value that is the cause of stress or frustration in your life. A friend or loved one might be making choices you don't approve of or decisions you don't think are right. Or they may have ignored your advice and decided to solve a problem in a way that you think is wrong.

In situations like this, when the source of your distress is someone near and dear to you, it can feel much harder to navigate your way through than when the cause of negativity is someone whose company you can take or leave.

When you find yourself in a situation like this, it is important to shift focus from your thoughts about the other person and back towards yourself. Ask yourself, 'Why is this bothering me so much?'

〰

*Everyone is free to make their own choices
in life and to follow their own path.*

If you find yourself feeling frustrated, stressed or worried about someone, it's important to recognise that these aren't negative feelings per se. They are feelings that are having a negative impact on you. And the cause of that negativity? It isn't the other person who is causing your negativity, it's coming from within you.

It's important to remember that these feelings, as unpleasant as they are, are coming from a good place. You wouldn't be feeling this way if you didn't care. And the more deeply you care about the person, the stronger feelings can be. The desire to push your point of view, force your perspective or intervene in some way can feel very strong, and the strength of this feeling can lead you to believe you *need* to intervene in some way. But in most cases the opposite is true.

If the person you care about is at risk of serious physical, mental or moral danger, then you should intervene in whatever way you can – they don't call the meeting of loved ones to encourage an addict to enter rehab an intervention for nothing! But most of the time, the things you may want to protect your friends and loved ones from are things like hurt feelings, financial losses, a career misstep or simply a lesson that you've already learned the hard way.

It is natural to want things to turn out well for the people you care about. It's completely normal to want them to succeed and to wish you could save them from pain – but it's not your job. It is not up to you to determine how any other adult should live their life. Their choices are theirs.

The good news is that most of the time things will turn out fine anyway, but even when it feels like you're watching a train wreck in slow motion, you won't help matters by being judgemental or trying to force a friend to take a different track. At times like this, remind yourself that while you might need to be there for the clean-up, it's not your job to pull on the brake.

✳ ACCEPT YOUR FRIENDS ✳ AS THEY ARE

Even your favourite people will have faults and imperfections, and while some of these traits might be an irritation, others are actually the flipside of a characteristic you really like or value.

During an argument with my husband in the earlyish days of our marriage, I made the mistake of saying, 'Stop being so sensitive!' He replied swiftly and wisely: 'You married me because I'm sensitive. Don't start complaining about it now'. I opened my mouth and then closed it. I opened it again, closed it and then decided to keep it closed – because he was absolutely right.

~~~

Don't judge your friends for their failings;
love them for their strengths.

Instead of devaluing your relationship by focusing on what the person is getting wrong, accept them as a whole person, and see their flaws as the small price to pay for all the things they are getting right.

✳ ✳ ✳

✳ NURTURE YOUR ✳ FRIENDSHIPS

Once you've decided that someone is a keeper – someone you believe has the potential to be a true kindred in your life – the next thing you need to do is give your relationship the support it needs to thrive.

One of the most nurturing things you can do in any relationship is to be generous. Generosity comes in many forms. It might mean being patient and listening when someone has had a bad day, or treating them to something nice when they're down on their luck.

Be generous, even with your forgiveness.

It's important to be generous with your forgiveness too. Holding on to a grudge is one of the most toxic things you can do, both to yourself and your relationships. In life, people will get things wrong, mistakes will be made and feelings will be hurt. While I'm not suggesting these things should be swept under the carpet, if you believe your relationship is worth salvaging, offer up your forgiveness as the very first step.

✳ ✳ ✳

✳ LOOK FOR YOUR ✳ KINDREDS

The author Richard Bach once wrote, 'Your friends will know you more in a minute than your acquaintances will know you in a thousand years'.

You don't need a hundred close and personal friends. You just need a few people who know you as well as, if not better than, the way you know yourself. Find them, cherish them and always hold them dear.

When it comes to friendship, it's quality,
not quantity that matters.

✳ ✳ ✳

MATTHEW'S NEGATIVITY DETOX

Except for a year travelling around Europe when I was twenty-two, I've lived in the same city my whole life. All my family are here too, and most of my oldest friends. I know lots of people, but Step 3 made me realise that not all of the people I spend my time with are 'my people' or even 'my friends'. I realise I spend way too much of my time feeling obligated to catch up with people for beers or to watch a game, just because we've known each other forever.

It's not that these people are bad or anything, but all we really have in common is that we went to school or university together and can rehash the same old stories and laugh at the same old jokes. The truth is, if we met now for the first time, we'd have barely enough in common to become acquaintances, let alone friends I see at least once a month.

I've recently accepted a new job in another consultancy. This is going to expose me to a whole new group of people. Before I start, I'm going to think about what I enjoy most in my friendships and what kind of people I prefer to hang out with. I'm going to use my new job as a chance to put what I've learned from this step into action and consciously look for some new friends.

I'm also going to permit myself to let some friendships drift ... while I don't need to ghost these people, or stop being 'friendly' when I see them, I'm going to stop feeling obligated to see them, because the truth is, we haven't been friends in years.

KEY INSIGHTS

STEP 3: FIND YOUR PEOPLE

1. Consciously choose your friendships. They are an investment, so make sure you invest wisely.

2. Not all friendships are forever – accept that seasons change, and friendships may change with them.

3. Your values will let you know if someone has the potential to be a true friend or just someone you are friendly with.

4. All friendships operate on a set of terms and conditions – be clear about yours.

5. Audit your address book. If you don't enjoy someone's company, stop spending time in their company.

6. It's not up to you to try and save your friends; your job is to accept them no matter what.

7. Don't expect your friends to be perfect – nobody is perfect, not even you.

8. Be generous with your forgiveness.

9. When it comes to your true kindreds, quality not quantity is key.

JOURNAL PROMPTS

1. Make a list of your true kindreds – not the people you see most often, but the people you feel most accepted and understood by. Next to each name make a note of why you choose to have them in your life.

2. Think about a friendship that has drifted. Put aside any hurt you may have felt at the time, and reflect on how the reason or the season for the friendship may have changed.

3. What is non-negotiable for you in a friendship? Make a note of your friendship terms and conditions.

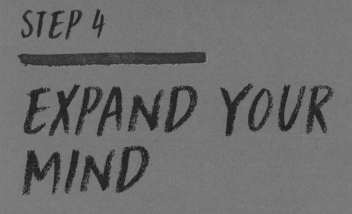

STEP 4

EXPAND YOUR MIND

Let go of unhelpful and outdated thoughts and beliefs, and develop new ones that serve you instead.

Limiting beliefs have the power to keep you stuck and to make you play small. When you liberate yourself from them you will discover your potential is far greater than you ever realised was possible.

Although I grew up in very comfortable circumstances, as the daughter of a hard-working first-generation Australian, I received really mixed messages about money.

There was an emphasis on earning it – the deep desire, common among immigrants, to work hard, make a new life, get ahead, and to ensure that each generation is more successful than the one before. My grandparents on my father's side came to Australia with very little and had to work hard for everything they had. There was an ingrained fear of spending money, or of it running out and having to start all over again.

These spoken and unspoken messages went something like: work hard, make money, don't spend it on yourself.

But these weren't the only messages I received. On my mother's side, my grandmother had married someone with a lower social standing than her and with considerably less wealth, and so the messages that filtered down from the maternal side of my family was not only that money doesn't buy happiness, but that wealthy people are unhappy. Perhaps this was my grandmother's way of making peace with her choice.

And so, I entered adulthood with the subconscious belief that I should work hard and make money, but also with the idea that people with 'too much money' (whatever that meant) were often unhappy. Like I said, mixed messages!

I would have never recognised these limiting beliefs or the potential they had to impact my life if it hadn't been for a wonderful opportunity I had in my early twenties to stay with an extremely wealthy family in New York. A friend of mine had nannied for this family and they had very kindly said to her that if any of her friends were ever passing through the Big Apple, they would love to put them up – they wanted to expand their daughter's perspective by making sure she met people from outside their privileged world.

It was my first trip to Manhattan, and I had no idea what to expect. Picture me, with my borrowed backpack, riding up to level 52; then imagine the look on my face when the doors of the elevator opened to an apartment that took up the entire floor.

I had never seen anything like this vast, luxurious apartment, but it wasn't the view that changed my perspective forever. I had grown up hearing subtle yet repeated messages that rich people were unhappy. But over the next four days, I realised that the things I had assumed were facts were actually just beliefs – limiting beliefs.

My hosts were incredibly generous, but more importantly they were kind. They were interested in me and my adventures and wanted to make sure I had a good time. I had never been surrounded by such wealth, but this family still radiated warmth, love and *happiness*.

On the second night, my hostess offered me a glass of champagne – good champagne – and we chatted about my first two days in New York. I don't remember what prompted the conversation to change direction, but she said, 'Domonique, I met my husband when we were both in college. I loved him before we had any of this' ... she gestured with her arms to indicate the spectacular 180-degree view ... 'but if you took it all away tomorrow, as long as we had each other and our daughter, I know everything would be okay'.

Her words were heartfelt, and the honesty was palpable, and I get goosebumps even now just thinking about it. The next night at dinner at a swanky restaurant uptown, my host said almost the same thing about his wife.

A few days later my backpack and I were in a limo on our way to JFK Airport and I knew my beliefs about money would never be the same again. You could be rich, seriously rich, and you could be happy. Properly happy. Living a life that was filled with love, where the money, while enjoyable, wasn't the main thing that was making you smile. My mind had been opened to my limiting beliefs and I was going to make sure that I never let it close again.

I also learned that you didn't have to save the good champagne for good; that you could drink it on a Tuesday if it suited you. But that's a story for another day.

✳ LET GO OF ✳ YOUR LIMITS

A limiting belief is a thought that holds you back: a belief about yourself or your life that limits your potential. These could be beliefs that have a direct impact on the way you approach things, like thinking 'I'll never get that promotion', so you don't bother to apply. Or they might be beliefs that have the potential to hold you back in a less direct way – like the belief I just shared about wealth being a source of unhappiness.

~~~

Whether you realise it or not, your limiting beliefs have been holding you back.

If you're not sure if you have limiting beliefs, just ask yourself the question, 'How do I hold myself back?'

Are you living your best life?

Are you realising your true potential?

If not, do you know why your current life isn't measuring up to your ideal?

Begin your search by looking within and understanding the role your beliefs have played and are playing in keeping you small and holding you back from doing, being or having everything that you want in your life.

We know there are some things in life that are well and truly beyond our control, but if your life is anything like the majority of my clients and the people who attend my workshops, then there's a lot more within your control than you probably realise.

You've just been letting your limits get in your way.

✳ FEARS ARE ✳ NOT FACTS

Despite the brake your limiting beliefs can put on both your potential and your confidence in pursuing that potential, sometimes they come from a good place. Your subconscious has a very strong desire to keep you safe: safe from hurt, disappointment, failure, embarrassment – safe from all of the risks that go with putting yourself out there and going after what you want in life.

But these risks aren't about life or death.

~~~

Your subconscious is trying to keep you safe – it's up to you to ask the question, 'Safe from what?'

Sure, if something goes wrong you might feel like you could *die* of embarrassment, and I know first hand how irrecoverable a heartbreak can feel, but recover from both you eventually do. But instead of understanding the complexities of the risks associated with any endeavour, your subconscious latches on to these risks and repeats them over and over like a playlist set on repeat. And eventually, your conscious mind accepts them as given.

But they're not facts, they're fears masquerading as facts. Don't let yourself fall for their disguise.

✳ FORGET THE ✳ RULES

While sometimes we are held back because our subconscious is trying to keep us safe, at other times we get in our own way because we're trying to stick to rules that are no longer valid in our lives. For example, perhaps as a child you were taught to always wait your turn. When you were in the playground or playing with your friends, this was important advice. Don't push in, wait your turn, everyone is going to get a turn eventually … If you have children, I'm sure you've taught them similar rules too.

While some of the rules we were taught in childhood may remain valid throughout our lives – don't lie, don't steal, don't cheat – not all of the things that we were taught back then are helpful to us as adults. If you have career ambitions, the last thing you want to do is politely wait your turn, hoping that someone notices you and gives you a chance to shine. Equally, when promotions are offered it is not the time to stand back and say, 'It's your turn, you go ahead of me'.

Not all of the rules you were taught in childhood serve you well in adulthood.

Growing up, you might have also received messages about how 'strong boys' or 'nice girls' behave. You might have been told not to cry, to put a lid on your emotions, or to be nice and not ask directly for what you want or need. But as an adult, if you want to have a deep connection with your partner and a strong, healthy relationship, being able to access your emotions, be open about your vulnerabilities and honest about your needs might be exactly the right things to do.

If you want to know what rules you're still following and which ones you need to update, take the time to examine your default response to any situation and ask yourself if this is still the best way or if there is a better way – age or situationally appropriate – you could respond instead.

✳ BREAK YOUR ✳
PROMISES

It's okay to break your promises; at least, sometimes it is. We make bargains with ourselves all the time; for example, if I eat a salad for lunch, I can have a cake with my coffee. Most of these internal 'deals' are of low consequence; the cake really isn't a problem unless you eat it every day, and these trade-offs are just part of how you navigate the comings and goings of your life.

But sometimes there are bigger things at stake, and the deal you've made with yourself is fundamentally important to your life. This deal is a commitment you intend to keep, like the wedding vows that promise to forsake all others, or an addict's promise to take one day at a time.

~~~

Not all of the promises you make need to be upheld forever.

Often the commitment or pledge you have made to yourself was fundamental in helping you through a challenging or difficult time, but now that particular time has passed, continuing to uphold that promise might actually be holding you back. For example, you might have told yourself that a promotion didn't matter as a way of managing the hurt you felt when you missed out. But that doesn't mean that all promotions don't matter, and you should never try for one again.

✹ GET CLEAR ABOUT ✹ WHAT YOU WANT

While the only thing really stopping you from achieving your potential might be you, that potential will be very hard to achieve if you have no real idea of what it is.

Through working directly with clients, workshop participants or coaching club members, I can confidently tell you that the reason why people don't have what they really want from life is almost always the same – they're not really clear about what it is that they want.

~~~

The only thing really stopping you from achieving your potential is you.

Sure, they might have a vague idea of what they're chasing: to find the perfect partner, to get their dream job or to get a whole lot richer, or slimmer or more successful overall. But what is missing from their quest is clarity about what this desired goal might really look like in their life. They waste their time and effort pursuing the wrong things, going in circles and never making any real progress because they're not sure what their next step really should be; or missing out on opportunities that are right under their nose because they never really knew what they were looking for.

If you don't know what you really want, you need to take the time to get clear; to rediscover your dreams, uncover your values and then to use them both to define a crystal-clear vision for your future.

✳ ✳ ✳

✳ BE HONEST WITH ✳
YOURSELF

You really can do, be or have anything you want in life, but the effort it takes to get what you want is often a lot more than people are willing to expend. If there are things you think or say you want from your life that you don't have, instead of thinking that these things only happen for other people or buying into the negative self-talk that says it's because you're not good enough, be really honest with yourself.

It might be that you want it, but you just don't want it badly enough. You might not want it enough to make the sacrifices, maintain the commitments or keep up with the effort required. This applies whether you've said you want to build an empire and haven't; if you've said you want to lose weight and be a healthier version of yourself, yet nothing has changed; or any other goal you say you want but haven't really made any real progress towards.

〜〜

Change requires effort and results take commitment.

There is no such thing as overnight success. Behind every success story you've admired from afar is a committed and consistent effort: doing the hard yards, showing up even when the going is tough and not giving up no matter how much you might want to. This is equally true for leaders in business, bestselling authors and sporting superstars as it is for everyday heroes like present parents, happy couples and people with fit and healthy physiques.

Success isn't achieved with a magic wand.

Sure, we'd all like to achieve financial freedom by winning the lottery – it's the easiest path to riches that there is! It's also the most passive and the least likely. There are much clearer paths to that goal or any other, but they require a whole lot more from you than just popping to your local store and buying a ticket.

If this is resonating with you in a rather uncomfortable way, don't hide from these feelings. Be honest with yourself and own up to what is really going on. Living your best, most brilliant life is going to take more than just creating a vision board – although I do love a vision board. No matter how clear your vision is, if you really want to have it, you have to be willing to work for it.

✳ IT'S OKAY TO CHANGE ✳ YOUR MIND

If you find yourself starting and stopping, or prevaricating and never really making headway, instead of beating yourself up or criticising yourself, take the time to understand what your inability to progress is really all about. Just because you like the idea of something doesn't mean you have to pursue it. I like the idea of being committed enough to train for a marathon, but I've long crossed it off my list of things I am likely to do.

~~~

*There is a big difference between being a
quitter and deciding to walk away.*

There is a big difference between quitting or giving up on something you really want, and consciously acknowledging that you don't want something nearly as much as you thought you did. Even if you're underway, or once you've started you find that it's too hard or not what you thought it would be, it's okay to change your mind.

It's time to be honest with yourself. Nobody wants to be thought of as a quitter, but there can be great relief in drawing a line under something that hasn't worked out and there's absolutely no shame in making the decision to walk away.

✳ LEAVE YOUR PAST ✳ FAILURES IN THE PAST

Just because you've tried to achieve something in the past and failed it doesn't mean that you're destined to fail at it forever, at least not if succeeding at it remains important to you. Whether it is a goal you've been pursuing or an internal change you are trying to make, if you haven't succeeded at it, it simply means you haven't succeeded yet.

When my clients lament that they're no good at something or tell me about a mistake they repeatedly make, I remind them that this is simply how things have been up until now.

~~~

Just because you haven't succeeded doesn't mean you never will, it just means you haven't succeeded yet.

When you find yourself thinking about something you're finding hard or a slip-up or error you've repeatedly made, don't reinforce your limiting beliefs and perpetuate a negative mindset by saying, 'I'm no good at this … ' or 'I always mess that up … ' Instead, switch your language to something much more empowering like, 'In the past, I found this difficult' or 'I'm still working towards that ...' It will be much easier to find the commitment you need to get back up and keep trying when you have the right mindset in place.

 YOU ARE WORTH IT

You deserve to live your best, most brilliant life – because you're worth it.

When I say this, I might be borrowing the tagline from a L'Oreal ad, but that line has been around for more than fifty years and outlasted so many other straplines and advertising messages because they are empowering words that we all need to hear.

You are worth it, and you do deserve it.
You just need to teach yourself to believe it.

✳✳✳

ASHLEY'S NEGATIVITY DETOX

Step 4 has been truly life-changing for me.

When I was a teenager, I was really creative. I was talented enough to be offered a scholarship to an art school, but my dad talked me out of taking it. He wasn't mean about my talent or anything like that, but he kept telling me there was no money to be made from art and if I became an artist I would struggle financially in life. I wasn't particularly academic, and he encouraged me to go to college to study typing, bookkeeping and all those essential business admin skills that he was certain would always be in demand.

And so I did. And my life hasn't been bad for it. My husband runs a building business, and when we got together I started working on the administration side, making sure quotes were sent out and invoices were paid on time. I know the skills I learned back at college have been an important part of our business success.

I've known for a long time that my father discouraging me from taking up the art scholarship was all about his limiting beliefs and his hopes (and fears) for my future. I'm sorry I was talked out of the opportunity, but I don't hold it against him ... I know he was doing the best he could to guide me to what he thought was a secure future.

But this step made me realise that not only did my dad have limiting beliefs, but I was holding on to his beliefs too. I have always had a range of art projects on the go as a hobby – I'm always drawing, painting or creating something. I've created portraits of all my friends' children, and they've been telling me for years that I should sell my artwork and start a business painting children's portraits.

I've always said 'no' and made excuses about being too busy, but I can see now that I've been holding the limiting belief that there is no money to be made in art, despite having numerous people offer to pay me for my work.

But not anymore, thanks to what I've learned in this step. I've decided to set up an Etsy store and am going to start creating portraits for people from the photos they send me. Who knows where it will take me, but plenty of people make money from their creative talents and I've decided that, from now on, I'm going to be one of them too.

KEY INSIGHTS

STEP 4: EXPAND YOUR MIND

1. Ask yourself, 'How do I hold myself back?' Then stop letting your limits get in your way.
2. Don't mistake your fears for facts.
3. Forget the rules of your childhood that don't serve you in adulthood.
4. Break your promises to yourself if they're no longer working for you.
5. Get clear on what you really want – it's impossible to achieve your potential if you don't know what it is.
6. Be honest with yourself – if you're not making any progress, maybe you don't want it as much as you thought you did.
7. Have the courage to walk away if you want to.
8. Leave your failures in the past, and focus on what you want to achieve in your future.
9. Remember that you're worth it.

JOURNAL PROMPTS

1. Identify any fears that you have been interpreting as fact. How can you reframe them so they stop getting in your way?

2. Think of something you have been saying that you want, but that you are not making any progress towards. Reflect on whether you really do want it or if it is not really as important to you as you had previously thought.

3. What would be different in your life if you let go of your limiting beliefs?

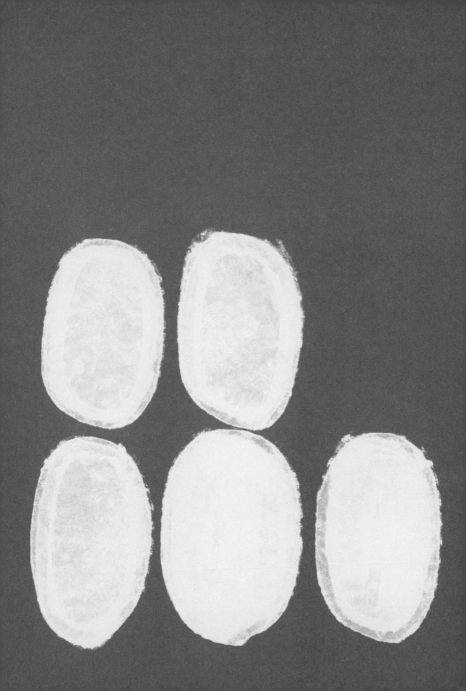

STEP 5

LOVE YOUR BODY

See your body in a whole new light and develop a much healthier relationship with it.

Your relationship with your body is no different to the other important relationships in your life. You need to nurture it if you want it to thrive.

In the novel *The Picture of Dorian Gray* by Oscar Wilde, Dorian makes a deal with the devil to stay young forever. The only thing that shows his true age is a portrait he keeps in his attic. Unlike Dorian, I never made a pact with the devil, and I don't have an aging portrait in my attic. But I do keep a pair of hotpants up there – to remind me of the wasted opportunities of my youth.

I bought these hotpants when I was twenty and working as a model. Although I never modelled high fashion – I was more of a commercials and catalogue girl – just like today there was a lot of pressure on models to be thin.

And I was.

Looking back at the photos from the time, I was tiny ... for me. But I'm not a naturally small build, I'm medium-sized, and although there was barely any fat on me, I was constantly being told by my agency that I needed to lose weight; that I wasn't skinny enough.

My hotpants weren't microscopic like the ones Kylie Minogue wore in her 'Spinning Around' music video, but they were still short shorts. And back then, I had the figure for them.

I just didn't appreciate it at the time. Every time I put those hotpants on, my eyes would zoom in on some perceived fault. A curve here, a dimple there, and I would decide that I didn't look good enough to wear them, and so I'd take them off again. In the end, I only wore them once, to a photoshoot ... but they did look good, and I have a picture to prove it.

But you could never have convinced me of it at the time.

I decided to retire gracefully from my modelling career when I realised that the only way to achieve the target weight the agency had set for me was to develop an eating disorder or a drug habit. Fortunately, neither option held any appeal.

Although I was in an industry that was highly critical of women's bodies, I actually wasn't any more critical of mine than my non-model friends were of theirs. That is to say that we were all extremely critical of what, with the wisdom of many years of hindsight, can only be described as the perfection of youth.

I never wore hotpants again, but a decade later, when I was in my early thirties, I went out one night wearing a dress with a plunging neckline. It wasn't indecent, but it definitely put my assets on show. When a friend commented that it was quite a different look for me, I confided in her that when I'd had the body for hotpants, I never wore them. I'd wasted that opportunity because I never thought I looked good enough.

I reflected with my friend that aging would most certainly have an effect on my body over time, but I was never again going to waste the opportunity to wear something I liked, while I still looked good in it. I wore that dress a few times and then moved on. But I'd made my point ... to myself.

But back to those hotpants. I showed them to my daughter not long ago and she said, 'I can't believe they ever fit you, Mum!' to which I replied, 'I can't believe I thought I was fat when they did'.

***

✹ DON'T WASTE ✹ YOUR YOUTH

I'm sure you've heard the expression that 'youth is wasted on the young'. Well, I don't think it just applies to the very young – children, teenagers or young adults – I think it applies to you and me too.

I am in the middle of my life. I tell my children that I am mid-century modern – sometimes in fashion, but always in style. Sometimes they laugh, and other times they just roll their eyes. But even in the middle of my life, I am younger this year than I will be next year. And I am much younger now than I will be in ten years' time. And so, I keep my hotpants to remind me to never waste my youth again.

~~~

Appreciate your body and the age you are right now.

What you do or don't choose to wear to cover your body isn't nearly as important as how you choose to feel about your body. Whether you are in your twenties and have noticed some fine lines, in your thirties and are beginning to see the effects of gravity, or you are like me and constantly covering up your greys, or perhaps wishing you had more greys to cover, whatever the changes you are experiencing in your body, the fact is you are aging.

It's inevitable.

But it's so much better than the alternative.

Instead of raging about the passing of time or spending endless hours and countless dollars trying to run from its effects, remind yourself that whatever your age, not only is constantly focusing on the negatives and feeling dissatisfied futile, in ten years you will look back on the face or body that you have today and wonder why you didn't appreciate it when you had it, and where on earth it went.

✳ ✳ ✳

✱ RESPECT ✱
YOUR BODY

As well as accepting your body even as it changes, I also want you to learn to show it a lot more respect. Pay close attention to the language you use when you speak about your body and the thoughts you hold about it in your head.

I caught up with a friend I hadn't seen for a few months and after we'd chatted for a while she remarked, 'I'm so fat; I'm disgusting at the moment'. My friend had gained a little weight, it was true, but there was nothing disgusting about her then, nor would there ever be. This gorgeous woman was a bit heavier than she wanted to be and yet she spoke about herself in the most hostile way.

~~~

Your relationship with your body is not that different to the other important relationships in your life. It needs to be accepting and respectful if you want it to thrive.

There really was no need to discuss her weight, but if my friend had wanted to bring it up there were so many healthier, more respectful things she could have said. She could have told me she felt uncomfortable at the weight she was or that she preferred her appearance when she was slimmer. She could have said she was concerned about her health or that she needed to kick some unhelpful habits. Or she could have confessed to me that she was worried that she would be judged for not maintaining her commitments to herself. There are so many things she could have said, but the words, 'I am disgusting' should never have left her lips.

I've included some affirmations to help you switch up the language you use when thinking about your body. Download the free workbook that accompanies this book. You can get it at domoniquebertolucci.com/negativity-detox.

✳ RESPECT EVERY ✳
BODY

While you are eliminating negativity by thinking about your own body respectfully, I want you to make sure that you show other people's bodies the same respect. Pay attention to the words you speak and the thoughts you hold about the people around you and even strangers in the street. If you have judgemental, critical or hurtful thoughts about other people's bodies, it doesn't mean you get off scot-free.

～～

Each time you are judgemental of someone else's body, your subconscious knows that the same thing could be levelled at you.

Even if the criticism itself doesn't apply – perhaps you're thin and the person you are judging is overweight – the fact that you are being critical, even silently, sends a very negative message to your subconscious. It tells your subconscious that being hostile and critical about someone's body is normal, and the next time you are judging your own body, your inner voice is less likely to stay silent and much more likely to pile on the criticisms instead.

✳ BE CLEAR ABOUT WHAT YOU ARE ✳ WANTING TO CHANGE

If your body is not the way you would like it to be, either through choices you've made or something else you can control, then by all means take the actions you need to change it. Lose weight, tone up, get fit; or if it fits within your values, have that nip or tuck. But once you've made those changes, make sure that you don't attach more meaning to those changes than they deserve.

~~~

When you change a part of your appearance, all that changes is that part of your appearance.

Losing weight won't make your life perfect, nor will developing a six-pack or buying a new set of boobs. Your body is yours; you are free to change it in any way you want, but don't overestimate the impact that change will have on your life.

✳✳✳

✳ CHOOSE HOW YOU ✳ SEE YOURSELF

Nobody's appearance is perfect, even those that you see in the media or online. Whether you think that photoshopping is an art form or tantamount to deceit, the safest assumption you can make is that nearly every digital image you ever see has been altered in some way. On those rare occasions that it hasn't, it has most likely been taken in perfect light, with an expensive camera, and with reflectors angled just the right way. Your reflection in your bathroom mirror simply can't compete.

Back when I modelled, it was said that the camera added ten pounds and a video added twenty … our main worry was our photos would make us look worse than we did. Nowadays, photo editing has been taken to a completely different level, but unless you are wise to the manipulation you can find yourself mindlessly accepting it.

I was watching one of my favourite shows recently featuring an actor who is around my age. She looked a bit different, and at first I couldn't work out why. Then it dawned on me: they had used a filter to smooth out the skin under her eyes.

It was subtle; if I hadn't been looking for it, I probably wouldn't have noticed it. But I'm so glad I did. Because of course, no matter what I do, what treatments I have, or how much I spend on various lotions or potions, my reflection will never be able to compete with something that has been digitally magicked away.

But accepting your appearance really shouldn't be based on what you see in the mirror versus what you see online because the reflection in your bathroom mirror isn't a true representation of you either. Unless your bathroom is set up like a photographer's studio, the light globes will probably cast unflattering shadows and your tiles might give off an unsightly glare. Your bathroom mirror probably isn't doing your reflection any favours either.

~~~

Train your eye to see things differently.

Instead, I want you to think about the way you see the people you love and care about.

If a friend of mine has gained weight I might notice the change in their appearance, but what really matters to me is did they gain weight because they have been having too much fun or have they been overeating to dull some sort of pain? Likewise, if they've lost weight, what I care about is if they were trying to improve their health or if their weight loss is the result of being too stressed to eat.

I never look at my husband and think, 'Gee, he looks rough' or 'Boy, is he getting old!' I appreciate his smile, I love the way his eyes sparkle and I'm glad his greys are finally catching up with mine.

My young son is fond of telling me that he loves my squidgy tummy because it was his home before he was born. When he describes my tummy as squidgy, he is NOT telling me I'm fat – he's telling me that he loves me.

Forget what you see in your mirror. The best way to see yourself is through the eyes of someone who loves you.

✳ YOUR SCARS ARE ✳ BEAUTIFUL

Some of the changes to your body will be gradual and happen over time. You might not even notice them happening at first until suddenly they take you by surprise. But other changes are far more instant, like the result of surgery, an accident or even the magic of giving birth.

~~~

Instead of looking at your scars and wishing you could make them disappear, realise that each scar is actually a celebration of how it came to be.

Maybe you brought life into the world, or perhaps you had a near miss or close call through injury. Whatever their cause, remind yourself that your scars are beautiful, and they are proof you have survived.

✳ ✳ ✳

✳ CHALLENGE YOUR ✳ BODY

Now that you're much clearer about how to appreciate your appearance for all that it is, I want you to proactively build a healthy body image by challenging your body and asking it to step up. It's time to remind your body what it is capable of.

When I hear people tell me they can't do something because they're old, I encourage them to reframe it – perhaps they're out of practice, or maybe they're just not match fit.

It is no secret that the communities where people live the longest have two things in common. The first is that these super-agers live in societies where age is valued, and the older they are, the more people look up to them and appreciate their wisdom.

The second thing about people in these communities is that they remain very active – they haven't used their age as an excuse to give up. They still climb mountains, work in fields and walk for miles.

∿

Set yourself a physical challenge, commit to it, and impress yourself with what you can still do.

While you might not be able to do the same things you were able to do at twenty-one, with commitment and practice you might surprise yourself.

INVEST IN YOUR FUTURE

If you want to live a long and happy life, you can't just make an effort with the happy part. You need to make choices that will help with the 'long' part of the equation too.

~~~

*You can't mistreat your body and expect
it to serve you long and well.*

Food and exercise fads will come and go but the things that remain are the same: eat everything in moderation, enjoy good-quality whole food and don't drink much more than a glass or two of wine.

Your body wants to be fed. But it also wants to move.

You don't need to be a gym bunny or fitness fanatic to make regular exercise a part of your life. Instead of meeting a friend for coffee and cake, you can meet for coffee and walk. Rather than eating your lunch at your desk and then browsing for news online, when you've finished your lunch take a walk and see what's new in your neighbourhood. Or pretend you are in Italy and take a *passeggiata* or casual stroll before or after dinner every evening.

People's capacity and ability for exercise varies. Some will need a lot of exercise and others not nearly quite so much, but everyone needs a bit.

✹ LOVE AND ACCEPT ✹ YOUR BODY

Your body is yours, and it's the only one you've got. If you want it to serve you well, treat it with love and respect. Nurture it with good healthful food, and strengthen it with regular exercise.

Accept that it is flawed and that your flaws are a part of what makes you, you. Don't place more value on your appearance than it deserves. While it might feel nice to receive a compliment on your appearance, how you look is not who you are.

Celebrate the fact that your body is yours.

Everyone has good days and bad days, fat days and thin days. Don't moan about the ravages of time or resent the passing of years. Instead, celebrate the fact that your body is yours – it has got you to where you are right now, and if you treat it right you have every chance of it getting you to wherever you'd like to go next.

✳ ✳ ✳

RACHAEL'S NEGATIVITY DETOX

This is a bit of an uncomfortable topic for me. I have three teenage daughters, so I know all about the importance of teaching them to be body positive and to always compliment their brains and personality and not just their appearance, but it turns out I've been giving them all the right messages while doing a terrible job of it myself.

Although I've made a point of not voicing it out loud, if I'm honest, every time I look in the mirror, I criticise myself and every time I eat cake or pasta, I berate myself. Every. Single. Time. I've been looking at my daughters' toned, trim bodies with envy and criticising mine for losing its youth – but I mustn't forget that I gave birth to those bodies. A lot of the changes in my body are at least in part because I brought them into this world.

This step made me realise that it's time to change. Instead of telling my daughters to love and respect their bodies while secretly hating my own, I'm going to practise what I preach. From now on, while I might not love my imperfections, I'm going to learn to be indifferent to them – they're not going to have the power to make me feel bad about myself.

I've also reminded myself that although I'm not as young as I once was, I'm certainly not old yet. For years I've been secretly fantasising about taking up jujitsu. Although my daughters think the whole idea of their mum becoming a ninja is a bit of a joke, I'm going to join a beginner's class and concentrate on impressing myself with what my body can still do.

KEY INSIGHTS

STEP 5: LOVE YOUR BODY

1. Don't waste your youth – you will never again be as young as you are today.
2. Your relationship with your body is no different to your other important relationships: it needs respect and acceptance if you want it to thrive.
3. Accept every body. It's just as unhealthy to judge other people's bodies as it is to judge your own.
4. Changing your body changes your body – don't expect it to change your life.
5. Change your perspective – see yourself through the eyes of someone who loves you.
6. See your scars as beautiful; they're proof you have survived.
7. Challenge your body, and impress yourself with what you can still do.
8. Treat your body well if you expect your body to serve you long and well.
9. Love and accept your body; it's the only one you've got.

JOURNAL PROMPTS

1. Think back to the criticisms you levelled at your body when you were younger. What would you like to be able to go back and say to your younger self?

2. Think of someone who loves you. How do you think they would describe your appearance?

3. Make a note of three things you could do to improve the way you treat your body and encourage it or your relationship with it to thrive.

STEP 6

PICK YOUR BATTLES

Consciously choose your conflicts – work out what is worth fighting for and when to just let go.

✳

Instead of fighting losing battles or trying to force things that are outside of your control, focus on what you can influence. Then take a deep breath and let go of all the rest.

You. Are. Not. In. Control.

Yes, I said that.

Trying to be in control, all of the time, is one of the biggest causes of stress for many people. Before we get into how and when to pick your battles, I want to focus on why so many of your challenges or battles might be occurring in the first place.

When I say that you're not in control, I don't mean to imply that your life is careening out of control like a runaway train – even though we all have days that feel like that. What I'm talking about is the desire that most people have to be 'in control' some, if not all, of the time. I believe this unrealistic desire is a huge cause of stress and unhappiness in so many people's lives.

The truth is, most of the time, you don't stand the slightest chance of controlling … well, just about anything.

✳ ACCEPT THAT YOU ARE ✳ NOT IN 'CONTROL'

There are very few things in life you can actually control: you can't control the weather, you can't control whether your train runs on time, if your flight is delayed or if you get stuck in a traffic jam. You can't control the people around you, the way your partner behaves or the way your children turn out.

Complaining when you're stuck in traffic or if your delivery is delayed isn't going to make a spot of difference.

~~~

There are very few things you can actually control.
As soon as you accept this, you will remove a
significant amount of stress from your life.

How often have you found yourself feeling frustrated at some form of bureaucracy or other administrative hoops you have had to jump through? Although the process may seem unnecessary or overly complicated, outside of writing a letter of complaint there is nothing you can do to change it. Allowing your frustration to take over is not worth inviting the stress it is going to bring into your life.

Next time you find yourself feeling frustrated by things that are outside of your control and can feel your frustration escalating towards anger or anxiety …

Stop.

Breathe in.

Breathe out.

And let go of anything that is not in your control.

It might not be right, it might not be fair, and it might not be how you would do it. But it is what it is, and in that moment, you need to accept that it's out of your control.

✹ RECOGNISE YOUR ✹ INFLUENCE

All is not lost, because while you may not have control over a person or situation, what you do have … is influence.

The best way to influence any situation is to ask yourself, 'What is the outcome I am trying to achieve?' You can't make your ideal employer hire you, but you can take the right courses, work on your resume, practice your interview skills, and make sure you're not running late on interview day. While you can't control whether or not you are ultimately selected for the job, there are a lot of things you can put your efforts towards that will ensure you're in with the best shot.

〜〜

When you focus on what you can influence, you give yourself the best chance of getting the outcome you want without exhausting yourself trying to force things that are outside of your control.

Likewise, if you're looking for a partner, you can give yourself the best chance of finding the right person by getting out and meeting new people and being clear on what you are looking for: your negotiables, your non-negotiables and your relationship values. That way you'll be able to recognise someone with genuine potential when they cross your path.

One area where your influence can have powerful reach is with children. As anyone who has children will tell you, they most definitely have free will. You can't control your children or *make* your children do anything. But you can set a good example by modelling the behaviour you want them to adopt. You can also encourage them with rewards or reprimand them or issue appropriate punishments so they learn that their choices have consequences.

When you learn to focus on what you can influence, you will get the outcome you desire at least *some* of the time.

✳ ✳ ✳

❋ DON'T FIGHT A ❋ LOSING BATTLE

Throughout life, you will have plenty of experiences that leave you feeling stressed, disappointed, frustrated, anxious or hurt, but when you engage in a losing battle you actively invite these unpleasant emotions into your life.

~~~

Your emotional resources are valuable – protect them by not engaging in pointless conflict or welcoming unnecessary stress and tension into your life.

Before you consider embarking upon your next crusade, ask yourself, 'What are my real chances? Do I have more than an eighty per cent chance of victory or am I fighting a battle that wisdom, history or past experience tell me that I'm not likely to win?'

If you think you are in with a good chance and that the reward will be worth the effort, then go for it. But if you assess that you'll likely lose but choose to engage anyway – in full knowledge of the stress or distress it might create – you need to have a good, honest think about what this conflict is really about for you.

If deep down you know that what is really driving your decision is the desire to be proven right, you might want to ask yourself if there are easier ways you can stroke your ego.

After all, your self-esteem is unlikely to benefit if you come off second best.

❋ ❋ ❋

✳ MAKE SURE YOUR BATTLES ✳ ARE WORTH FIGHTING

People are often drawn into a losing battle because they feel infuriated and want things to be right – 'because they should be'. While in a utopian world this would be a worthy goal, you really need to think about whether you're actually going to make a difference, and if the difference you're likely to make is going to be worth your while.

I ask myself, 'Why am I getting into this fight? How important is this fight and do I have a good chance of winning? And will the emotional or financial gain outweigh the negativity this situation will bring into my life?' If I conclude that it is not healthy for me or worth engaging, the final question I always ask myself is, 'Am I going to be able to find peaceful acceptance of this situation?' After all, there is no point in deciding not to fight if you are going to continue to complain!

But sometimes there are battles that, while you may not feel confident you can win, you feel you have to fight regardless. Perhaps you believe that even if you don't win, your contribution will be part of a larger effort, or maybe you feel that the only way to honour your values or moral code is to march on regardless.

If this is the case, then even though it might be a losing battle, holding your ground and standing up for what you believe in is most definitely the right thing to do. At times like these, you need to focus your energy and your emotional resources on the fact that you are fighting this battle to stand up and be counted and to have your voice heard. But you also need to remove any attachment you have to victory. This doesn't mean you don't want to win. It just means that your happiness won't be contingent on winning and that your sense of gratification and fulfilment will be achieved by knowing you fought a good fight.

~~~

Engage yourself in the fight, but detach
yourself from the outcome.

Early on in my career, I experienced exactly this kind of battle. My boss was both bullying and harassing me. Each time I raised my concern with my manager and later the human resources manager, I was told I needed to put up with the situation or find another job. That was not a good response. Or legal one – or at least so I thought.

The stress of my boss's behaviour eventually became overwhelming and I began having physical symptoms including hair loss and stomach pains. When my GP suggested I go on sick leave, I decided enough was enough; this 'illness' had a very specific cause – so I went to see a lawyer.

I shared this story in more detail in my book *The Happiness Code*, but the short version is: I didn't win. I didn't even get to fight. The organisation I was working for had diplomatic immunity. That meant unless an employee committed a capital crime – murder, manslaughter or something along those lines – an employee would not be held accountable for their actions in a UK court of law.

My lawyer did a great job, but after twelve months of tribunals, courts and appeals the time came to accept that my employer's immunity would not be waived, and I would never get the chance to bring my case to court. It wasn't an easy time in my life, but I had gone into this with my eyes wide open – I had *engaged* myself in the fight but *detached* myself from the outcome.

I knew that I had won all I needed to win, many months before. I was still an employee the day my legal papers were served. All I had ever wanted was to say, 'Your behaviour is NOT okay', and the look on my boss's face when he received his summons told me my message had been received loud and clear.

It was an incredible journey, and despite losing the battle, to even have the legal battle, knowing I had made myself heard, was worth it for me.

✳✳✳

✳ ALWAYS REMEMBER ✳ TO FIGHT FAIR

One side of my family is Italian. On that side of the family, voices are often raised, and issues are hotly debated, but no matter how heated a discussion is or how passionate an argument becomes, it is never reduced to being *about* the person – the focus always remains firmly on the issue.

Growing up, I was taught that while it is important to stand up for what you believe in, it is equally as important to never say anything that you can't take back. I can remember when I was quite young my dad explaining to me that words were not weapons, they were tools and that no matter how sorry you are, once your words are out there you can never get them back.

~~~

Never forget the importance of dignity – yours and that of the person you're arguing with.

When you do need to go into battle, regardless of who it is with, make sure you fight fair – never mock or belittle someone, don't intentionally hurt them or attempt to manipulate their emotions. And always, always keep your focus firmly on the issue, and behave in a way that means, regardless of the outcome, you can still hold your head up high.

✹ DESCRIBE YOUR EMOTIONS INSTEAD ✹ OF DEMONSTRATING THEM

I speak to many people who have never learned how to be angry or to disagree in a healthy and respectful way. They bottle up their feelings and then feel nothing but guilt and remorse when they explode. Or they get so worked up when they have to raise a problem that it escalates into an argument that never needed to be had. By allowing their feelings to drive what they are saying and the way they are saying it, they end up creating a lot of unnecessary negativity in their lives.

~~~

When you lose your temper, the fallout can often outweigh the relief.

While losing your temper or exploding can feel good in the moment – like a high-pressure valve that finally has the chance to be released – the consequences can be far reaching.

There is a much better way to communicate your displeasure, disappointment or frustration in a truly empowering way. Don't demonstrate your emotions; describe them in a calm quiet voice.

Simple, non-inflammatory language is the most effective:

I am feeling deeply disappointed …

I feel very hurt …

I feel like crying …

I feel disrespected …

When you do feel angry, while you could lose your temper and scream or rant and rage, your message will be received far more powerfully if instead of raising your voice, you lower it and say calmly and quietly, 'I feel so angry I could scream'.

✳ FIND YOUR ✳
VOICE

Being able to state your case, firmly but not aggressively, is one of the most important, confidence-boosting skills you can develop. But for a lot of people, women in particular, it is also one of the hardest.

Many people misunderstand what being assertive is and shy away from it. They think they may be regarded as rude or disagreeable or simply as not being 'nice'. But asking for what you want or need, politely but firmly, doesn't make you rude or disagreeable, it simply makes you someone who has a clear understanding of what they want or need. And anyway, nice is a hugely overrated virtue – especially when it's being used as shorthand for 'doesn't rock the boat'.

When you stand up for yourself, whether that means letting the waiter know that your meal has been served cold, asking for what you need in a relationship or calling out someone who is treating you disrespectfully, you are reinforcing your self-esteem. Being meek doesn't serve you. When you stay silent and take it on the chin you are complicit in the erosion of your self-esteem.

〰

When you are assertive you are saying 'my wants and needs matter' and by extension 'I matter'.

The first time you're assertive, it can be quite a surprise to find that the world doesn't end. Don't get me wrong, the other party might not like what you have to say, and they might let you know it. But it won't kill them to hear it.

What you learn by being assertive is that you can survive someone being unhappy with you and what you've had to say. The experience might not be pleasant, and you might not enjoy it, but those inconvenient feelings will pass, and you will end up feeling so much better for standing up for yourself.

✳ ACCEPT THAT YOUR CHOICES ✳ HAVE CONSEQUENCES

It's important to recognise that every single decision you make has consequences, and there is no point expending your energy resenting them. They are what they are. You need to understand and accept the impact your choices will have on your whole life, not just the specific thing they relate to. You don't have to like it, but you do have to accept it.

〰

Your choices and decisions will always have consequences –
make sure you are willing to accept them.

If you are not willing to accept the negative or less desirable impacts of your choice, then you need to re-examine your options and see if there are other alternatives you feel more comfortable with.

✳ ✳ ✳

❋ DON'T FIGHT THE SAME ❋ BATTLE TWICE

Avoiding or hiding from conflict rarely has a positive effect but spending your life in a constant cycle of conflict is not healthy – mentally, emotionally or physically. While some conflict is necessary, you need to make sure you're not having the same argument over and over again.

We all know a relationship, be that a romantic couple or a group of friends, where the same argument is being played out over and over again. Sometimes the specifics will differ, or the details might change, but the essence of the argument always remains the same.

Make sure this doesn't happen to you.

If you are unhappy about something or have an issue that you need to raise, bring it up calmly and assertively. Then commit to standing in your power until you can, at the very least, make some progress with your concern.

You don't need to resolve every issue or argument entirely the first time it is raised. In fact, it can be counterproductive to try to do so. While the sentiment 'never go to sleep on an argument' is sweet, all too often it just means that things get swept under the carpet just so people can go to bed.

Instead of dusting things over or hastily putting the lid back on Pandora's box, focus on making even the smallest bit of progress and then next time the issue comes up pick up where you left off. Or calmly commit to revisiting the matter in a day or two.

*Frequent conflict is exhausting, but craving a
conflict-free life is not healthy or realistic.*

Rather than fighting every battle or remaining silent, make
the decision to consciously choose empowered conflict and
move any issues forward step by step.

✳ ✳ ✳

ALYSSA'S NEGATIVITY DETOX

I'm a lawyer; resolving battles is what I do for a living, but this step made me realise that I haven't been very discerning about what battles I've been fighting in the rest of my life.

At work, my conflicts have very strict professional parameters. Did one party fail to meet the terms of their contract? If so, what's the remedy? I'm paid to be like a dog with a bone and to not let go until my client gets some, if not all, of what they need. I like my job and I'm good at what I do, but somehow I've fallen into the habit of letting it take over the rest of my life. Not just in terms of workload, but I can see now that the way I approach a breach of contract has started to become how I approach every conflict in my life ... and it's just not necessary.

I've realised that I don't need to win every personal point just because I am right in principle. So often it's just not worth the energy. While there are some principles that are really important to me and that I'll continue to speak up about, like being anti-racist or respecting LGBTQI+ rights, I'm going to stop trying to convince everyone to think my way about things that don't matter in the scheme of things.

I think deeply about the things I believe in, but I know not everyone does. A lot of people mindlessly accept what they read or repeat ideas they've heard elsewhere without thinking about it for themselves. But this step has helped me to accept that's their loss, not mine.

As a lawyer, I enjoy a good debate, but I can see now that not everything needs to be one – it just gets exhausting. So from now on, I'm going to make a point of letting go a lot more.

KEY
INSIGHTS

STEP 6: PICK YOUR BATTLES

1. You are not in control – don't cause yourself unnecessary stress and frustration by kidding yourself that you are.
2. Focus your energy on what you can influence and the outcome you're trying to achieve.
3. Don't waste your energy fighting a losing battle.
4. Be clear about what you are really fighting for – know what you need to get out of it and how you'll know if it's time to walk away.
5. Always fight fair. Make sure your conflict is always about the issue and never about the person.
6. Describe your feelings, don't demonstrate them.
7. Being meek doesn't serve you – learn to be assertive and find your voice.
8. Don't go into battle with yourself. Accept that your choices have consequences and that you might not like them all.
9. Never fight the same battle twice – stand in your power until you can at least move one step forward with it.

JOURNAL PROMPTS

1. What have you been trying to control that, on reflection, you really have no control over at all? How are you going to think differently about this from now on?

2. Are you engaged in any conflicts that are using up too much of your energy or that you find yourself regularly engaging in? Reflect on how you could change your approach.

3. When do you find it most difficult to be assertive? What can you do or say differently to help you to find your voice?

STEP 7

CHOOSE YOUR FAMILY

Decide which relationships you
want to invest in and which ones
you're happy to let drift away.

You deserve to be loved unconditionally, appreciated for all that you are, and to live the life that you want to be living. Nurture your relationships with people who want all of this for you and more.

When I was twenty, I moved out of my family home and across the country to Sydney. I had a grand vision of taking on the world, and although I was totally unprepared for what the world was going to throw at me – aren't we all at twenty? – I felt fearless and full of hope.

Over the years I retained a strong connection with my hometown, Perth, and went back for Christmas, weddings and other significant occasions. But the truth is, at the end of each visit, as I passed through the departure gates and onto flight QF-whatever, I never once so much as glanced back over my shoulder after I'd said goodbye. I always felt so excited about what I was heading towards that I really didn't give any thought to what I was leaving behind.

Or at least I didn't … until the first time I visited Perth after my daughter was born. After that visit, as I walked through those departure gates, it felt like my heart was being torn right out of my body. The pull was so strong, and at first I didn't know what the feeling was, it was so unfamiliar to me.

As the tears pricked my eyes, this time I stopped, baby strapped to my chest, and turned to wave goodbye one more time. It hit me then. I was leaving my family. And not only was I leaving my family, I was also taking my daughter away from hers.

I cried all the way back to Sydney. Not just for that farewell, but for all those careless and carefree goodbyes in the seventeen years that had gone before.

As I sat through that flight, sniffling into my tissue, I questioned how I had ever been able to leave my family behind. And then the answer dawned on me. Although I had left the family of my birth in Perth, I had been creating and re-creating my sense of family everywhere I went … with friends who had become family – my chosen family.

I realised I hadn't been living without my family.

I had just been living apart from *this* family.

❋ DON'T ACT LIKE ❋ A CHILD

When I first left home a neighbour said to my mother, 'You must really miss her I bet you wish she'd come back'. My mum, always very wise, replied to this well-meaning comment, that of course she missed me – it already felt like someone had cut off one of her limbs … Missing me was natural. But she hadn't had me so that I would grow up to be her companion, so no matter how much she missed me, she would concentrate on being excited for me and for what lay ahead.

If you want to have a healthy and mature relationship with your parents, the first step to adulthood is to cut the invisible cord that ties you to them. You need to make the decision to no longer act like a child or accept being treated like one.

Before you were born, you were physically attached to your mother. As a baby you were dependent on your parents (birth or adoptive) for absolutely everything. But a healthy and mature parent–child relationship changes over the years. It grows and evolves as you move through your childhood, your tricky teenage years, and then on to becoming an adult yourself. Those ties that held you so tightly to your parents loosen, and parental influence stops being so important, so all-encompassing.

At least that's what should happen.

Except people are complicated, and both you and your parents are human. Even the best-intentioned parents will get things wrong, and I see many people come into adulthood troubled by complicated relationships with their parents.

The more childlike you allow your role in the relationship to be, the harder it will be to live as a fully empowered adult.

In an ideal world, your relationship with your parents would be one where you are each able to respect each other as adults, while recognising that many years ago those older adults were responsible for raising you. The challenge I see for many people is balancing the awareness that for the rest of their life they will be their parents' child, while remembering not to behave like one.

Please don't think I'm suggesting that there is anything childish about having a complicated or conflicted relationship with your parents. But the more childlike you allow your role in the relationship to be, the harder you will find it is to live as a fully empowered adult.

✳ ✳ ✳

✳ STOP WAITING FOR ✳ PERMISSION

Your parents may have brought you into *their* world, but their responsibility was always to help you to get ready to go out and create your *own* world. In whatever shape or form that might be. This is what it means to grow up.

It's unfortunate that so many parents failed to read that page of their parenting instruction book. Except of course, they didn't have an instruction book. Yes, there are hundreds of different parenting books out there, but there is no one official manual or guidebook that comes with the job, and even parents with the best intentions are bound to get some things wrong.

But as their children, so do we.

I regularly hear from my clients and people who attend my courses that they're worried about what their parents will think; that they're not going to approve of their choices, or that their parents are going to hate it if they do (or don't do) something. This would make more sense if I was talking to kids, but these are fully grown adults – many of them with children of their own.

~~~

You do not need a permission slip from
your parents to live your life.

You might prefer it if your actions were met with parental approval, and you might long for their unconditional love and support, but as an adult you don't need to wait for their approval or to convince them that you are going about things in the right way.

If you want your parents to treat you like an adult, you need to start behaving like one – and that means backing yourself. Part of being a functioning adult is having confidence in your decisions and not holding yourself back if your plan meets with parental doubt.

✳ YOUR MISTAKES ARE ✳ YOURS TO MAKE

As an adult, you alone are responsible for your choices.

Most parents are very good at telling their children what to do. From the mundane (and exhausting) – wash your hands, eat your veggies, hurry up or you'll be late for school – to those much bigger lessons about what is right and wrong.

When you were a child, it was appropriate that your parents were guiding you and directing you. You needed them to teach you what to do and how to do it – whether it was learning manners, or how to read, or how to make an apology or find a way to tell someone you care. You needed their guidance and support to work out what was right and how to amend or adjust your approach along the way because you didn't have the experience or know-how to work it out on your own.

But you're not a child anymore.

~~~

Whenever you make a decision, it is yours to make.

As a fully fledged adult you get to decide what to do and how to do it – all on your own. Most of the time you'll get it right, but even when you get it wrong, remind yourself that it was your mistake to make.

✳ OWN YOUR ✳
VALUES

I hear many stories from people about feeling pressured by their family to do, be or act in a certain way. If you don't want to feel pushed or pulled into someone else's vision for your best life, it's important to revisit your values and put boundaries in place based on them.

You don't owe your family, and your family doesn't own you.

Constantly trying to argue your corner or justify your decisions is exhausting, and when it is essentially your idea versus someone else's it is virtually impossible to deliver the winning shot.

But if you're able to make your point or state your case and then clearly articulate the values your choice or decision is based on, you'll find that while the people in your life still might not agree with you, it will become harder for them to argue with you.

✳ ✳ ✳

✳ STAND UP FOR ✳ YOURSELF

Creating an adult relationship with your parents will be easier if you first examine how you and your family members communicate with each other. If your parents, or for that matter your siblings, are constantly telling you what to do, criticising or judging your choices, or regularly putting you down, it's time to call it out.

They might not be aware they're doing it; it might just be a bad habit or perhaps it's the way their parents treated them. Maybe they're just being careless in the way they're expressing their views. But no matter what the reason is, it's time for you to stop patiently waiting for them to change.

~~~

Past behaviour is the best indicator of future behaviour.

Instead of setting yourself up for frustration and disappointment by expecting things to be different to the way they've always been, make the decision to be the one to take a different approach. If you feel your parents are regularly criticising you, it's time to find a way to say, 'Please don't speak to me like that'.

When I first moved to Sydney, my mum missed me but was excited for me, but my dad – my Italian papa – just wanted me to come home. I would chat with my parents on the phone each Sunday and Mum would want to know all about what I was doing and how it was all going. But my dad only had one question for me: 'When are you going to come home?'

I'm pretty sure the thousands of kilometres between us emboldened me a little, but after several months of this, I decided to call Dad out on it and explain what it really felt like to be asked that question week after week. Kindly but firmly I said, 'Papa, I know you love me, and I know you miss me, but I am over here, trying to achieve something that's really important to me. Every time you ask when I'm coming home it feels like you're asking me if I've failed yet. I love you very much but if all you want from these calls is to find out if I've failed then I'd really prefer it if you just didn't call.'

Dad was shocked, but I had made my point loudly and clearly. He heard it.

I never did move back, and I know he still wishes I would. But he has learned to respect that I am living my life and even though living in another city is not what he would have wanted for me, he chooses instead to be happy for me.

✳ ✳ ✳

✳ TEACH PEOPLE HOW YOU ✳ WANT TO BE TREATED

Just because your parents are older than you, it doesn't mean they always know better than you. You need to be prepared to teach them how you want to be treated.

When you don't like what your parents have to say and you wish they would just bite their tongues, instead of filling up with anger or allowing your resentment to build, reverse your roles and explain to your parents how you would like them to speak to you.

Just because your parents are older than you doesn't mean that they know better than you.

If you consistently apply this approach, over time they might learn how to change, and your relationship will evolve and be in a much better place. And if they don't, at least you will know that you gave them every chance.

✳ PUT CLEAR BOUNDARIES ✳ IN PLACE

Sometimes, even though you were born into the same family, there are family members you just can't find common ground with. If, after explaining how you would like to be treated, putting clear boundaries in place and articulating which values are important to you, you find that you're still being treated in an unacceptable way, it is okay to make the decision to walk away from that member. And as an adult you get to decide how far you want to walk.

If it's someone you care about and still want to spend time with, you might just need to be vigilant about which conversations you engage in when you are with them. If you don't want to be justifying yourself or defending your opinions all the time, just limit your conversation to simple and superficial things like films you have seen or books you have read.

~~~

It's okay to make the decision to walk away.

But if you feel like you've tried everything you can and the only way forward is to create a long or permanent separation, that's okay too. You don't need to feel guilty or force yourself to stay, just honour your values, respect yourself and hold your head up high as you walk away.

✳ FORGIVE YOUR ✳
PARENTS

One of the most important things you can do for your own wellbeing to is forgive your parents for the various ways they may have failed you and to recognise that, for better or for worse, they were likely doing the best they could.

If, like me, you were fortunate enough to have good parents, parents who didn't get everything right but tried as hard as they could, forgiving their failings is an easy enough thing to do. But if your parents didn't even attempt to make the grade, whether they were abusive, harmful or just absent in their role, I still encourage you to work towards finding it in your heart to forgive them. You might want a therapist's help to do this.

True forgiveness isn't about trying to make someone else feel better or telling them it's okay. It's accepting that what has happened has happened, and then releasing yourself from a future filled with hurt, anger or hate.

〰

Forgiving someone is something you do for you.

✳ CREATE A SENSE OF FAMILY ✳
IN YOUR LIFE

Although you can't choose the family you were born into, you *can* choose the family you surround yourself with. It doesn't matter if these people are your blood relatives or not.

Your chosen family might be a big extended family filled with third cousins twice removed. It might be one but not all of your siblings, or a step-parent who cared for you in a way you wished your own parent had. Your family might be a group of friends you went to university with and now have an inseparable bond, or really any combination of the above.

Surround yourself with people you cherish.

While these people, whomever they are and however you've found them, may not always be members of your family of birth, they are your family *of choice*. They are people who, regardless of time, distance or circumstance, will cherish you and love you for life.

Love them back.

✳✳✳

STEPHEN'S NEGATIVITY DETOX

My mum has always been a difficult person. She'll be the first to tell you that she's had a hard life, and it's true she has, but whether she realises it or not it feels like every time I see her, she is intent on making sure that my life is hard too.

Exploring this step has made me see that this probably isn't going to change – I'm nearly fifty and my mum has been criticising me and putting me down for as long as I can remember. Instead of hoping that she would stop and doing everything I can to keep her happy I've decided to accept that this is just who she is.

It's been a really hard decision to make, but I've decided that I need to take a step back in my relationship with her.

I'm not saying I'm going to abandon her, but right now everything is on her terms. I see her every week, call her every day, and for what? So she can put me down and criticise me some more. I've decided I need a whole lot more time and space between calls and visits. While I'll always love my mum – she's the only mum I've got – I realise that a lot of the time she doesn't behave in a very likeable way. It's time for me to start to protect myself from her negativity and put-downs by being around them less often.

It's important for me to remember that I'm not threatening withdrawal or doing this to force her to change – I'm creating space so that I can take care of myself and protect my energy and self-esteem.

KEY
INSIGHTS

STEP 7: CHOOSE YOUR FAMILY

1. Stop acting like a child and don't accept being treated like one.

2. It's time to grow up. You do not need a permission slip from your parents to live your life.

3. It's your life – you get to decide how you want to live it.

4. You don't owe your family, and your family doesn't own you – don't let anyone try to convince you otherwise.

5. Don't wait patiently for things to be different – ask for the changes you need.

6. Reverse the roles, and teach your parents how you want to be treated.

7. Put boundaries in place, and don't be afraid to walk away if you need to.

8. Forgive your parents – release yourself from any hurt, anger or hate.

9. Surround yourself with your chosen family – supportive people who know you better than you know yourself and will love and cherish you for life.

JOURNAL PROMPTS

1. Reflect on the role you usually adopt when you are
    with your parents/family members. What can you learn from
    your current approach and how might you improve your
    relationship(s) if you adjusted your approach?

2. Where do you need to establish clearer boundaries with your
    family? How can you communicate those boundaries in an
    honest, respectful and mature way?

3. Make a note of the people whom you are closest to – your
    chosen family. Why have you chosen them?

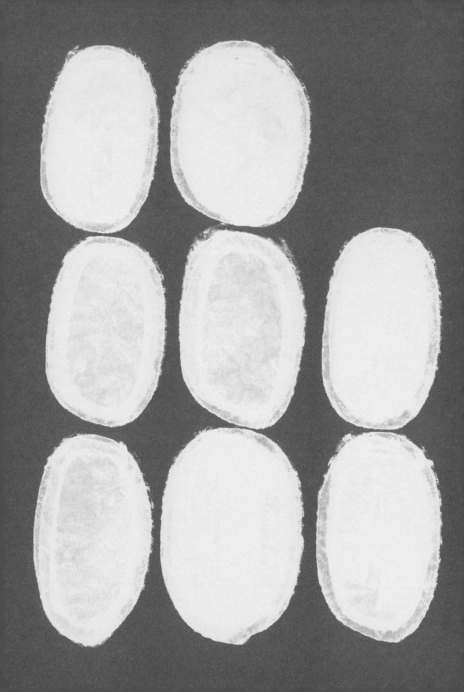

STEP 8

BE YOUR BOSS

Learn how to take charge and
focus on what you really want
from life, so you can actually start
to achieve it.

✳

You deserve to be living a happy and fulfilling life, one that is filled with joy and where you are deeply satisfied with all that you have and all that you do.

While I now look back and lightheartedly call it my quarter-life crisis, my twenty-fifth year was a pretty miserable time in my life.

Whenever someone asked me how I was, I always said 'fine'. And the truth was, things did look good on the outside: I was in a well-paid corporate job, with a nice house, nice car and nice boyfriend. But I felt like I was living someone else's life and that my success was two-dimensional.

I didn't want my life to be just 'fine'.

I remember crying to one of my closest friends that I'd thought my life would be so much better than *fine* by that point ... that I'd thought it would be *fabulous*. And the truth was, it was anything but. I was working for a bully in a job I hated, ending a relationship I never should have started and deeply angry with myself for not being in possession of the perfect life I had been so sure would have been mine.

Eventually, I worked out what 'success' really meant and how I wanted my life to be. Over time I made a whole lot of changes: career, relationship, the works. I learned that my life didn't need to be fabulous – like something from the pages of a magazine – it just needed to be happy and fulfilling to me.

Life was good.

But living a happy and fulfilling life is not a once-and-done proposition. Nearly twenty years later, I realised that my life had started to feel 'fine' once again. And just like before, there was nothing wrong with it ... at least not from the outside. But deep down I knew that I'd stopped pursuing some of my ambitions, put some of my biggest dreams on hold and shoved some of my hopes to the side. I did this while I got on with the busy work of taking care of my life: my family, my relationship, my clients. I wrote books, I did the laundry – life was full!

Looking back, I can see that I was trying to do all the things I did well, and somewhere in that fullness – in playing all my roles well – I'd stopped paying close attention to what I really wanted from my life.

I knew it was time to make changes and that I needed to get my life back to being much better than fine. But I also wanted to make sure that I didn't sacrifice, compromise or put at risk any of the things that were working in my life. And so, I followed the exact same process I teach – I went back and explored my dreams, examined my values and came up with a new vision for the future I wanted to create.

✳ OWN YOUR ✳ CHOICES

Many people feel frustrated, resentful and even angry at the life they find themselves living. But the truth is, most people would rather live with those deeply unpleasant feelings than actually do anything about changing them.

~~~

If nothing changes, nothing changes.

Sometimes it can feel easier to stay where you are in life – to blame other things, other people or say that you have no choice – rather than to challenge your status quo and explore other alternatives. You might even feel like a part of you is secretly comfortable stuck at a dead end – it might be cosy in your cul-de-sac.

If you find yourself feeling this way, remind yourself that it's *your* life; you don't have to change it if you don't want to. But if you decide to leave things the way they are, you must choose to accept them as they are.

If you find yourself believing that you don't have any choice, remind yourself that there is always another path you could be taking. It might not be the one you want to take, and you might choose not to take it, but there are always other options.

When you fully explore your options and consciously choose your circumstances, your sense of contentment with your situation will increase.

✳ HONOUR YOUR ✳ VALUES

In her poem 'The summer day' the Pulitzer Prize–winning poet Mary Oliver asked, 'What is it you plan to do with your one wild and precious life?'

This is such a powerful question and the good news is there is no one right answer to it. You have so many options available to you, and what matters is that you come up with the right answers for you.

Growing up, as someone who loved to talk and could hold my own in an argument, people often suggested I should be a lawyer. In my father's eyes becoming a lawyer was the pinnacle of career – no, make that life – success but it was never what success was going to look like for me. That didn't mean I knew what it should look like instead.

Back in my quarter-life crisis, I spent hours agonising about what I was going to do with my life. There were so many options, and the pressure to get it right felt overwhelming.

I wish I knew then what I know now.

I wish I'd known that you shouldn't waste time doing what you think you should be doing or chasing ideals you think you should be chasing. That instead you need to take the time to discover what really matters to you and design your life based on your dreams, values and ideals.

There is no *one right path* for you to follow.

There are so many different ways you can create a happy and fulfilling life, so instead of pressuring yourself to find the one perfect path, make choices that honour your values. Make choices that feel right for you, right now.

~~

When you explore your values, you will realise how many different paths have the potential to be the right path for you.

By far the most common thing I hear, when I teach people about values, whether it's people who've bought my Personal Happiness Prescription course or students in one of my in-depth coach training programs, is that they've never really given their values that much thought.

They know where they want to go on holidays, what car they'd like to drive or what brand of jeans they prefer to wear. But they've never really thought about their answer to the question, 'What matters most to you in life?'

You get to choose what you are going to do and how you are going to live your life. While part of that choice might mean that you need to ignore or reject the ideas everyone else has for your life, it also means working out what you actually want.

If you want to be the boss of your life, you need to create a vision based on your values, and then find both the courage and commitment to bring that vision to life.

✳ HAVE A CLEAR ✳ VISION

Looking back at how I got to where I am in life, I know I've made several choices that to other people might have seemed wrong at the time. I ended a relationship with a good man who loved me; I turned down multiple job offers and promotions; and I walked away from what is now a billion-dollar company to start a new career.

But each time I walked away I knew what I was walking towards.

~~~

Have a clear vision – it's the only way you'll
know if you're heading in the right direction.

I didn't have the precise coordinates, but armed with a clear vision and a real awareness of my values I could easily tell whether or not I was going in the right direction.

You won't always get it right, and more than once I've wished for a pair of hindsight goggles of my own, but unless you take the time to work out where you really want to head, you don't stand a chance of getting there.

✳ MAKE THE RIGHT ✳ COMPROMISES

Making choices based on your values creates a solid foundation for a truly happy life, but even with a crystal-clear vision you need to be prepared to make compromises along the way.

~~~

Every choice or decision you make will have consequences. You need to own your choices and all the consequences of those choices.

I often speak with people who are feeling frustrated, dissatisfied and unhappy in their lives, but when I listen to them, I can clearly hear that they are ignoring, rebelling against or resenting the consequences of the choices they've made. They might have chosen to move to a larger house, but now feel frustrated because their life is constrained by their mortgage payments. Or maybe they made the decision to work part-time when their children were young, and now feel resentful that their career is not as dynamic or progressing as rapidly as it once was.

When you make compromises without aligning them with your values, or even considering them, you end up feeling *compromised*. But when you make decisions that are aligned with your values, while you might not enjoy some of the compromises you have to make, you'll be able to take comfort in the knowledge that these concessions are a part of your bigger picture. Remind yourself that the decisions you're making are taking you closer to, not further from, your best, most brilliant life.

✳ DON'T BE AFRAID TO DISRUPT ✳ YOUR STATUS QUO

The real reason most people aren't making the changes they want and need to make in their life is fear. You've probably heard people talk about fear of failure, and you might have even heard people talk about fear of success, but the fear I am talking about here is more subtle, more insidious.

It's the fear of disrupting your status quo.

Life is a delicate balance. The more you have to juggle, the harder it is to keep all those balls in the air. You might find yourself feeling worried that pursuing your goals, hopes and dreams will compromise or sabotage other things that are important to you – things that *are* working in your life.

~~~

You don't have to sacrifice the things that are working in your life in order to fix the things that aren't.

Living a happy and fulfilling life doesn't have to be an all or nothing equation. I believe there's a sweet spot. Sometimes the changes you need to make will mean doing more, other times it might mean doing less, but if you focus on finding that sweet spot between pursuing your vision and honouring your values, the life you create will be the one you really want to be living.

✳ START SMALL AND ✳ KEEP GOING

Now that you know that you need to get clear on your values and design a vision for your future, I'm guessing that like most people, you've discovered more than a few changes you need to make.

The idea that you are not where you want to be in life and that you might need to make some changes can feel overwhelming. Let me reassure you that you don't need to make all of those changes at once. And you definitely don't need to start with the biggest change first.

In fact, sometimes it's the smallest changes that can have the biggest impact on how you feel about your life. Other times it might be the cumulative effect of a series of smaller, consistent changes that gets you to where you want to go.

~~~

You don't need to change everything all at once, and you don't need to know all of the answers before you begin.

Instead of spending hours creating a complex and detailed plan for your perfect life, I want you to ask yourself, 'What is one simple thing I could do that would make me feel a little bit better about how things are?'

And then I want you to go and do it.

✳ WILLPOWER IS ✳ OVERRATED

It is very common for people to say that they lack the willpower to stick with the changes they want or need to make in their life. But I believe willpower is overrated. Strength of will – willpower – is sometimes necessary, it's just not quite as important as you think it is.

When you want to make a change in your life, focus your attention on creating helpful habits and ditching any unhelpful ones. Be diligent in this. Any time you catch yourself thinking, 'I don't have the willpower' or 'I'm just not disciplined', substitute that unhelpful thought with, 'What new habit could I create that would help me stay on track?' Sure, you will still need a little bit of discipline to embed your habit, but pretty soon it will become natural and normal to you.

Think about it when was the last time you left the bathroom without washing your hands, felt comfortable leaving the house in the morning without brushing your teeth or any of your other personal hygiene preferences? You do these things naturally and without thinking, but it wasn't always that way. When you were a small child someone had to remind you to do these things several times a day, but now that you're an adult they're something you never give any thought to at all.

The same is true for any other new behaviour you want to adopt. You might need structure, reminders and discipline to get you started, but once you're on your way, you'll find that you won't need your willpower nearly so much, because your habits are doing most of the heavy lifting for you.

Helpful habits are the key to creating
lasting changes in your life.

✳ ✳ ✳

✳ DON'T BE DEFEATED ✳ BY YOUR GOALS

Now that you know how important your habits are, it is time to stop beating yourself up when you don't achieve your goals. Be a little kinder to yourself.

I'm not anti-goal. Setting a goal and achieving it is an exhilarating feeling. But the truth is, most people fail to achieve their goals most of the time – and it doesn't feel good. Indeed, it can feel crushing.

I believe the how, when and why we've been taught to create goals is fundamentally flawed. The majority of the time, when we set goals they are simply a best guess of what is possible. Yet we hold ourselves accountable to them as if our success was guaranteed, that no deviation is permitted, and the only explanation for any resulting failure is ourselves.

I call this the Goal Myth, and I believe it's a major cause of unhappiness for many people.

〜〜

Expecting yourself to achieve your goals,
just because you've set them, causes you
stress, erodes your self-esteem and ultimately
leaves you feeling bad about yourself.

If you want to put an end to the success/failure struggle you've been having with your goals, shift your focus away from your goals as the be-all and end-all, and put them back in their rightful place – as just one of the many tools you can use to help you get what you really want.

✳ ✳ ✳

LIVE AN INTENTIONAL LIFE

If not goals, then what?

Instead of setting goals, I want you to ask yourself, 'What do I want to say about this? How do I want to feel?', and use your answers to these questions to create clear intentions for your life – to create your 'why'.

There is no one right way to live your life. What looks like the dream life for one person could be a vision of hell for someone else. What matters isn't that you live a perfect life, it's that you live the life that's right for you – it's that you live an *intentional* life.

I feel so strongly about this approach – this shift in focus from goals to intentions – that I developed an entire process around it called the Intention Method™ and now I train people in how to apply it to their own life and how to teach others to change their approach too.

When you focus on your intentions – and have a clear sense of your 'why' – you will feel much clearer about what you really want to achieve, feel much more confident about pursuing it, and find it easier to stay completely committed to the inspired, motivated actions you need to take to get it.

What matters isn't that you live a perfect life, it's that you live an intentional life.

LYNDITA'S NEGATIVITY DETOX

The lessons of Step 8 have been really interesting, although not entirely comfortable for me. I made the decision a long time ago not to live a conventional life. I didn't want to follow a career path or get married and settle down with children. I wanted to travel the world and live an exciting life and so I designed my career to make that possible for me.

As an independent IT consultant, I get paid well, I can work from anywhere in the world and have lots of time off for holidays and travel between contracts. I'm respected for my knowledge and for a long time I felt like I had it made. But my ego got a bit of a jolt recently when a friend who came through university with me received a 500 000-dollar bonus. I'm paid well, but not that well! It really threw me, and I wasn't just feeling envious of her massive payday, but properly green-eyed about her corner office and the long-term investment banking job that provided her with it. I found myself questioning my own career choices and worrying that I'd failed or let myself down in some way.

I've been in a funk about it for a little while, and I was beginning to wonder if I was having a premature mid-life crisis or at least a mid-career one, but this step has helped me to get clear on what was going on for me.

My friend and I started out on the same path, but we've made very different choices along the way. I love the positive consequence of my choices – the freedom, flexibility and all the time off I get. While I've been enjoying these benefits, my friend had been toiling away in the same company, investing time and money in an MBA and taking holidays only if or when she was allowed. While her half-a-million-dollar bonus was the upside of her choices, the flip side of mine was that I would never be in the running for one.

Now that I realise what was going on for me, I feel like I can be genuinely happy for my friend. I know we're on different paths, but I've also realised that I'm not fixed to mine and if I want to change direction or follow a different path, I can. I'll make sure I'm clear about what the trade-offs will be if I do.

KEY INSIGHTS

STEP 8: BE YOUR BOSS

1. Own your choices. Be honest with yourself about the life you really want to be living.
2. Honour your values; they are your unique prescription to a happy and fulfilling life.
3. Have a clear vision; it's the only way you'll know if you're heading in the right direction.
4. Make sure your compromises are aligned with your values – that way you won't feel compromised.
5. Don't be afraid to disrupt your status quo.
6. When it comes to making changes, start small and keep going.
7. You don't need willpower – you need helpful habits.
8. Don't be defeated by your goals. They're just one of the many ways to get what you want.
9. Live an intentional life.

JOURNAL PROMPTS

1. Are there any consequences to the choices you've made/are making that you've been feeling angry or resentful about? How can you reframe these frustrations?

2. What compromises are you willing to accept as you take a more values-based approach to your decision making?

3. What new, helpful habits do you want to create to support you in creating your best, most brilliant life?

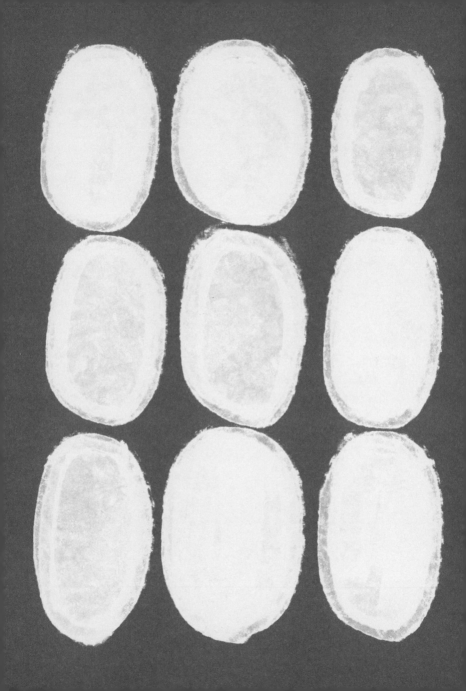

CELEBRATE YOURSELF

Break the cycle of endless self-criticism, lift yourself up when you're feeling down, and always see nothing but the best in yourself.

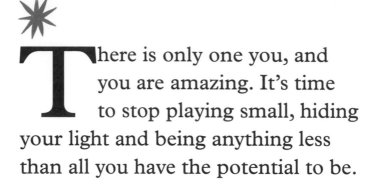

There is only one you, and you are amazing. It's time to stop playing small, hiding your light and being anything less than all you have the potential to be.

Like many people, I was bullied as a child.

I've parked this experience mostly in the recesses of my memory, bringing it out only occasionally – like when I'm asked about it in an interview or briefly in my book *The Daily Promise*. But like anyone who has experienced trauma, the scars are still there. And sometimes they catch you by surprise.

A couple of years ago I realised I'd been living my life as if my personal dimmer switch was turned down. I realised I hadn't been stepping into my full potential and that I had been holding myself back. Ouch!

As a coach, I like to make sure I'm always walking my talk, so I didn't want to ignore this uncomfortable discovery or sweep my feelings back under the carpet. And so, I sat with them, and journalled, and sat with them some more.

As I dug deeper and deeper into my soul, the cause of it all came to me. Just as I had done when I was ten years old, I was hiding my light. I was avoiding being seen and I was protecting myself. There was no lightning bolt moment that led me to realise this, just a series of smaller revelations that may not have meant much individually, but that collectively illuminated a pattern of choices I hadn't even known I'd been making.

But once I could recognise these revelations for what they were, I felt like I was watching a slide show from the seventies – except my slide show was not a series of somewhat dull holiday photos; instead, with each click, I saw another time when I had played small, hoped to be asked, or waited patiently for a turn that hadn't come.

From the outside you never would've known – I'd written bestselling books, flown high in the corporate world, ran my own business and was married with a happy family. I'd achieved a lot. But this wasn't about the things that I'd done. It wasn't even about the things I hadn't done; it was about *why* I hadn't done them, and who I might've become if I had.

As I looked back on more than thirty years of adult life, I could clearly see those moments when I hadn't let my light shine, when I hadn't stepped into my brilliance ... and when I hadn't given myself permission to be all that I had the potential to be.

Moments when I had let myself play small.

I knew then and there that while hiding my light had played a role in my past I wanted no part of it in my future.

✳ *STOP PLAYING* ✳ *SMALL*

Your first pledge to yourself, as you learn to celebrate yourself, is to make the decision to stop playing small and to stop holding yourself back from all that you have the potential to be.

Not playing small doesn't mean you have to do something in the public eye – write books or speak on stage in front of thousands of people like I do – although if that is what your potential feels like to you, then you should definitely go for it.

What I'm talking about is that nagging doubt at the back of your mind – the one that keeps asking, 'Is this as good as it gets?' And you know you've been playing small when that question is immediately followed by either a sense of guilt for wanting more or the desire to apologise for not being satisfied with what you've got.

〰

Step up and step into all that you have the potential to be.

I want you to stop ignoring yourself or hoping this feeling will go away. It won't. From now on, I want you to make the commitment to stop playing small and instead step up and step into all that you have the potential to be.

✳ ✳ ✳

✳ SILENCE THE CHAT ✳ INSIDE YOUR HEAD

In any life there will be plenty of people who put you down, criticise you or say and do things to encourage you to play small. It's so important that you're not one of them.

When you are striving for growth or trying to improve your performance, it's all too easy to fall into the destructive habit of being your own worst critic. Everyone has a little voice in their head that is chattering away constantly. I wonder what kind of conversation is yours having?

Are you generous, encouraging, inspiring and motivating; or are you critical, judgemental and downright mean? Or perhaps your little voice is actually a big bully, constantly putting you down, criticising your efforts and telling you that you're not good enough.

〜〜

Stop engaging in endless self-criticism. The only thing it will change is how you feel about yourself.

Your subconscious is very simple. It doesn't evaluate messages, weighing them up for accuracy or usefulness; instead, it just regurgitates the information it has received as fact – what goes in comes out. Every time you say to yourself, 'Geez, I'm so stupid!' your subconscious believes that you *are* stupid.

If you want to maintain a healthy level of confidence and self-belief, you need to put a stop to these messages and take back the ownership of the chat inside your head.

✳ BECOME YOUR OWN ✳ BEST FRIEND

Not only do you need to stop being negative towards yourself, what you really want is for your internal dialogue to be actively positive – cheering you on like your best friend would.

~~~

Harsh, critical or sarcastic communication has no place in your life, especially when you're the source of it.

The language and tone you should be using is warm, encouraging, positive and supportive – the kind of language you would use any time you were hoping to bring out the best in someone.

When I make a mistake or get something wrong – even if it's something like forgetting to do something I've told myself I need to remember – my favourite response to myself is: 'I'm really good at other things' and that, instead of 'Idiot!', becomes the phrase on repeat in my head.

ACCEPT YOUR MISTAKES

Not everything in life will go as smoothly as you might hope. Making a mistake or an error of judgement and wishing you hadn't is part of being human and in no way deserving of the internal flogging far too many people give themselves for it.

~~~

You are going to make mistakes, and that is okay.

Nobody can get everything right all of the time, and making mistakes is an important part of how we all learn, grow and become better versions of ourselves.

If a friend told you a story about how they had really messed something up or blown an important opportunity, you would probably find yourself commiserating and then saying whatever you thought your friend needed to hear to help boost them back up again.

You need to take this approach with yourself too.

Have a moan for a moment, let out your frustration or disappointment and then move into confidence-repair mode.

Nobody is perfect.

Instead of focusing your attention on a mistake you've made, switch your attention to all the things you're getting right.

✳ RISK ✳
FAILURE

Once you've accepted that you're not perfect and that mistakes are a natural part of life, it's time to build your confidence right up.

One of the best ways to build unshakeable confidence is to step outside your comfort zone – regularly. Stepping outside your comfort zone is like giving your sense of self a shake-up.

It's easy to become complacent and accepting. You may say with a shrug, 'I'm good at this' and 'I'm not good at that', but how do you really know what *more* you're capable of if you never try?

Risking failure is not about placing yourself in a position where you might lose everything you have or injure yourself terribly. But you and I both know that a life in which you are completely safe and nothing ever challenges you or makes you uncomfortable is unlikely to be your best, most brilliant one.

When you hear the saying, 'Do one thing each day that scares you', the idea isn't to be afraid for your safety and wellbeing. It refers to the things that scare you in an emotional sense – things that place you at risk of failure or disappointment, but at the same time take you one step closer to your dreams.

*The more you risk failure, the more your
subconscious will believe you're a success.*

Every time you step out of your comfort zone you send a
clear message to your subconscious that says, 'I wasn't afraid to
try'. Your subconscious receives this message as a sign of self-
belief and gives your confidence a boost.

✳ BE PROUD OF ✳
YOURSELF

The next thing I want you to do, as you learn to celebrate yourself, is to commit the sin of pride.

Sort of.

When we are young, most of us are encouraged not to brag, boast or do anything else that can be seen as big-noting – and with good reason; behaving like this can be really unattractive. Bragging or boasting is about comparing yourself to others. It's about saying I am more than you; I'm better, smarter or richer than you.

Comparing yourself to someone else is never helpful. Even if you are sure that you are the smartest, richest or best, it's only a matter of time before someone else comes along and knocks you off your perch.

But the flipside of this learnt modesty is that most people don't know how to comfortably and confidently acknowledge their best efforts because they're so busy trying to make sure that they don't brag.

~~~

Celebrating your success is acknowledging that
you have been the very best you can be.

Celebrating your success is not about comparing yourself to others or celebrating a win at someone else's expense. It simply means being proud of yourself.

Your real friends want you to succeed, and when you're positive and enthusiastic about the progress you're making it's exciting for the people around you. But if you're still feeling shy about your success, don't worry. You don't *have* to involve anyone else at all. You can celebrate your success quietly and privately, just by taking a moment to acknowledge how hard you have worked, how far you have come and all that you've achieved along the way.

✳ ✳ ✳

✳ DEVELOP AUTHENTIC ✳ CONFIDENCE

One fear that clients raise again and again is that they don't want to become 'overconfident'. They're worried that if they improve their confidence, they might appear arrogant and overbearing.

Authentic confidence is never arrogant or overbearing.

Overconfidence or arrogance is a symptom of fear and inadequacy. On some level, people who are arrogant or overconfident are usually making up for a deep, ingrained fear that they really aren't good enough at all.

Real confidence, on the other hand, isn't about being better than anyone else. It's about knowing you are being the best *you* can be. When your confidence is authentic, not only does it radiate from you like a brilliant golden glow, but it actually lifts others up and sweeps them along in your brilliance.

✳✳✳

✳ LEARN TO TRUST ✳ YOURSELF

Now that your confidence is beginning to grow, I want to remind you how important it is to trust yourself.

Life is filled with choices and it takes courage to make a decision, rather than just drift along.

Some people feel that, before they can make a decision, they need to canvass all their friends and loved ones for their opinions to ensure that they're making the right one.

Asking for help or support can be a sign of strength, but not when you are using it as a way of eliminating your fear of getting something wrong or as a way of outsourcing your decision-making to others.

There are no guarantees in life, and it's a mistake to think that by getting everyone else's input, you are reducing your risk of getting something wrong. In actual fact, you're probably compounding the situation – the more you listen to other people, the harder you make it to listen to yourself, trust your instincts and know the right answer for you.

~~~

The more you trust in yourself and are strong in your decisions, the more your confidence will increase.

As I've said before, there are no right or wrong decisions.

As long as you knowingly and consciously make a decision, it will always be the right one for you. Of course, as time goes on, more information may come to hand and you might discover that another alternative might have been the better one.

Hindsight is a wonderful thing. With the wisdom of hindsight, there are lots of things I might have done differently, but those experiences will have to remain things that I can learn from, not things that I'll live to regret.

✳✳✳

✳ GIVE YOURSELF PERMISSION ✳ TO SHINE

True self-belief comes from having innate confidence – confidence in who you are, not just in what you can do. It is about believing in yourself, your character, your strengths and knowing that as long as you focus on being the best you can be, you *are* being the best you can be.

〜〜

Innate confidence is about truly believing in yourself, without justification, simply because you're you.

Giving yourself permission to shine means believing in who you are and all that you have the potential to be. And it means believing in your right to fulfil that potential. I want you to believe in yourself, in your dreams and in your right to pursue those dreams, and I want you to give yourself permission to do, be and have all that you can in life.

I began this chapter by sharing a story about how I realised a few years back that I had been hiding my light and being less than all I had the potential to be.

This realisation didn't create an instant change in my life, at least not from the outside. There were plenty of things I was really happy with, and I wanted to be conscious about any changes that I made.

Once again, it wasn't about being reckless, it was about being truly intentional.

There was unlearning and relearning.

There was trial and error, pain and patience.

But in the end ... there was light. My light.

And that is my wish for you.

I hope that as you've detoxed your mindset and eliminated the negativity from your life, that your light is now ready to shine brightly too.

NATALIE'S NEGATIVITY DETOX

I feel completely confident in the work my consultancy does and the results we get for our clients, but this step made me realise that I don't really feel that way about myself. I often feel like I've got to where I am by luck. Of course, 'right time, right place' plays a role in every success, but deep down I know I'm good at what I do and that I play a big part in why our clients keep coming back ... I just find it hard to remind myself of this.

If I've taken one thing away from this step it's that I need to be proud of myself and all that I have achieved. It was so good to be reminded that being proud of myself won't make me obnoxious or turn me into one of those pushy types I wanted to get away from back when I decided to start my own business.

I know it's good leadership to share the limelight with your team, but I think I've become so good at it that I end up keeping myself in the dark. I've been hiding from the spotlight and making sure I don't draw attention to myself.

But I've decided I want to change that and that I do want to celebrate myself. I'm going to think of appreciating my strengths as a personal development challenge. I'll start a list and add to it all the time. I'm going to encourage our staff to do this too.

I know that when I step more fully into my identity as the founder of this business and acknowledge the role I've played in all of the success that we've had, it's going to be good for me and for our bottom line. I'm sure as I put into action what I've learned in this step and allow my reputation to grow, rather than being a 'best-kept secret', even more success is going to come our way.

KEY
INSIGHTS

STEP 9: CELEBRATE YOURSELF

1. Stop playing small – step up and step into all you have the potential to be.
2. Stop being your own biggest critic – take back the ownership of the chat inside your head.
3. Become your own best friend.
4. Accept your mistakes, and see them as a chance to learn and grow.
5. Risk failure – stepping outside of your comfort zone will help you to feel like a success.
6. Be proud of yourself.
7. Develop authentic confidence – commit to being the best you can be.
8. There are no right or wrong decisions, so learn to trust yourself to make the right one for you.
9. Believe in yourself and give yourself permission to shine.

JOURNAL
PROMPTS

1. Can you identify any aspects of your life where you have been playing small? What will you do differently in future?

2. Make a list of at least three things you can do to step outside of your comfort zone. Next to each item, make a note of the date that you commit to taking this step.

3. What would be different in your life if you truly gave yourself permission to shine?

A FINAL WORD FROM DOMONIQUE

Now that we are at the end of this book, I want to thank you for coming on this journey with me. More importantly, I want YOU to thank yourself for going on this journey.

It will always be easier to have an ordinary life, and as I said right back when we started, most people are 'fine' with fine and 'okay' with okay.

I'm so glad you're not.

I'm so glad you decided to show up and learn how to detox your mindset and eliminate negativity so you can make living your happiest and most fulfilling life your reality.

You deserve to live your best, most brilliant life – not just someday, every day – and by applying the lessons you've learned in this book, I'm confident you're well on your way.

PS: I'd love to know what your biggest insights and your favourite mindset shifts have been throughout *9 Step Negativity Detox*. You can find me on Instagram or Facebook at domoniquebertolucci; pop on over and say hello and tell me what is different for you now that you've begun to detox your mindset and eliminate negativity from your life.

PPS: If you never got around to downloading the workbook created to go with this book, you can still access it free at domoniquebertolucci.com/negativity-detox. I've included summaries of each chapter, exercises and expanded journal prompts to help you go deeper, plus a few extra goodies.

ACKNOWLEDGEMENTS

My first thanks go to my wonderful agent, Tara Wynne at Curtis Brown, without whom I might still be dreaming of publishing a book some day.

Thank you to Pam Brewster, Brooke Munday and all the team at Hardie Grant for giving my books such a welcome home. To Regine Abos for creating the gorgeous design that brings this new Mindset Matters series to life. To my editor Kate Daniel for balancing a light touch with a careful eye, for making sure that I always make sense and for doing so with such warmth and good humour. Thank you to Karen Yates and Stephanie Van Schilt for helping me to bring the original concept to life.

To my readers who connect with me in my Facebook group and on Instagram, thank you for sharing your experiences or simply stopping by to say hello. I am thrilled that you have invited my words into your world, and it makes my day when I hear all the different ways you have been putting them into action in your lives.

To Holly Kahmal for sharing my vision and helping me bring it to life.

To Sophie, Esther, Kate, Anna, Valerie, Antonia, Fiona, Francesca, Ruby, Kat, Annie, Alice, Charlie and all my other Belleville friends. I never imagined when I said goodbye that I would have to stay away for this long. I miss you and can't wait until we can have coffee, drink wine and enjoy endless conversation once again.

After all those goodbyes it filled my heart to welcome new friends into my life. To Penny and Rob, Paris, Indi and Daisy. There isn't anyone I would rather be stuck in lockdown next door to. And to Carrie, Siobhan, Gadia, Nicole and Louise, for helping me to fill the gap that my London girlfriends left.

To Claire for the last ten years and Sam for the last fifteen. To Brooke for nearly twenty and Polly for twenty-five. To Jane and Sophie for the last thirty, Callie for the last forty and Mary for the best part of fifty years. And to Alecia, Tristan, Adele, Liz and Sarah for more collective years than any of us would care to count. I know without a doubt that I will continue to choose you again and again, for the rest of my life.

To Mum and Dad, Jeff and Julie, Josh and Lara, Lisa and Tony, Isabelle and Benjamin, Genevieve, Aileen and Mike, and Nancy and Barry. You can't choose your family, but if you could I know people would be lining up around the block to choose mine. Thank you for so many things that it would take another book to list them all.

To my darling Sophia and precious Toby, thank you for being the shining lights in my life. Every time I think that I couldn't possibly love you more, it always turns out that I do. And to Paul, for nearly twenty-five years of love and laughter. Thank you for everything, always.

ABOUT THE AUTHOR

Domonique Bertolucci is the bestselling author of *The Happiness Code: Ten keys to being the best you can be* and seven other books about happiness: what it is, how to get it and, most importantly, how to keep it.

Domonique has spent the last twenty-five years working with large companies, dynamic small businesses and everyday people, teaching them how to get more happiness, more success and more time just to catch their breath.

Prior to starting her own business in 2003, Domonique worked as a model and then in the cut-throat world of high finance, where she gained a reputation as a strategic problem solver and dynamic leader. In her final corporate role, she was the most senior woman in a billion-dollar company.

Domonique's readership spans the English-speaking world, and her workshops, online courses and coach training programs are attended by people from all walks of life from all around the globe: people who want more out of life at home, at work and everywhere in between.

As well as being an accomplished professional speaker, Domonique is the host of three top rated Audible Original Podcasts. She has given hundreds of interviews across all forms of media including television, radio, print and digital media; more than 10 million people have seen, read or heard her advice.

When she is not working, Domonique's favourite ways of spending her time are with her husband and two children, reading a good book and keeping up the great Italian tradition of feeding the people that you love.

Domonique jokes that she has nearly as many passports as James Bond. She is Australian by birth, Italian by blood and British by choice. She is currently based in Sydney, Australia.

OTHER BOOKS BY DOMONIQUE

The Happiness Code: Ten keys to being the best you can be
Love Your Life: 100 ways to start living the life you deserve
100 Days Happier: Daily inspiration for life-long happiness
Less is More: 101 ways to simplify your life
*The Kindness Pact: 8 promises to make you feel good about who you
    are and the life you live*
The Daily Promise: 100 ways to feel happy about your life
*You've Got This: 101 ways to boost your confidence, nurture your
    spirit and remind yourself that everything is going to be okay*
*7 Step Mindset Makeover: Refocus your thoughts and take charge
    of your life*

GUIDED JOURNALS BY DOMONIQUE
Live more each day: A journal to discover what really matters
Be happy each day: A journal for life-long happiness

FREE RESOURCES

You can download a range of free tools, templates and extra resources designed to help you to live your best, most brilliant life at domoniquebertolucci.com/life.

KEEP IN TOUCH WITH DOMONIQUE
domoniquebertolucci.com
facebook.com/domoniquebertolucci
instagram.com/domoniquebertolucci

Join Domonique's private Facebook group for regular discussion, insights and inspiration to help you get more out of life.
Facebook.com/groups/domoniquebertolucci

FOR MORE INFORMATION
Find out more about Domonique's
life coaching courses and programs:
domoniquebertolucci.com/programs

Find out more about Domonique's training, certification and corporate programs:
domoniquebertolucci.com/training